Built *on* Values

creating an *enviable culture* that outperforms the competition

Ann Rhoades

with Nancy Shepherdson

JOSSEY-BASS
A Wiley Imprint
www.josseybass.com

Published by Jossey-Bass
A Wiley Imprint
989 Market Street, San Francisco, CA 94103-1741—www.josseybass.com

Jossey-Bass books and products are available through most bookstores. To contact Jossey-Bass directly call our Customer Care Department within the U.S. at 800-956-7739, outside the U.S. at 317-572-3986, or fax 317-572-4002.

Jossey-Bass also publishes its books in a variety of electronic formats. Some content that appears in print may not be available in electronic books.

Library of Congress Cataloging-in-Publication Data:

Rhoades, Ann, 1944-
Built on values : creating an enviable culture that outperforms the competition /
Ann Rhoades with Nancy Shepherdson.
p. cm.
Includes bibliographical references and index.
ISBN 978-0-470-90192-2 (hardback), 978-0-470-94990-0 (ebk), 978-0-470-94989-4 (ebk),
978-0-470-94988-7 (ebk)
1. Corporate culture—Case studies. 2. Success in business—Case studies. 3. Values—Case studies. I. Shepherdson, Nancy, 1955- II. Title.
HD58.7.R524 2011
658.4'063—dc22

2010043039

Printed in the United States of America

FIRST EDITION

HB Printing 10 9 8 7 6 5 4 3 2 1

CONTENTS

FOREWORD

By **Stephen R. Covey,** author of *The 8th Habit: From Effectiveness to Greatness*

I have believed in what Ann Rhoades is doing since we met at a conference where we were both speaking years ago. We both heard echoes of our beliefs in the other's words, a belief that people matter and can be inspired to do great things. What Ann Rhoades has done with this book, producing a blueprint for values-based cultural transformation, meshes completely with those ideas. In order to be successful in a volatile world, you must unleash the goodwill and creativity of your people. You must organize your culture in a way that will help your people achieve great things without constant supervision from above. Set this up right, and people will astonish you regularly with their great ideas and ability to take your organization to a higher level.

Built on Values shows exactly how to organize your culture to make that happen. It is a practical guidebook for transforming an entire organization or just your little corner of the world into a place of caring and passion. Ann's Values Blueprint process shows a clear pathway to harness the best impulses of your people to accomplish a wholesale transformation of the way you do business. By aligning all of your processes—hiring, rewarding, leadership, metrics, communication—with values that are meaningful and profound for your people, you can reinforce the idea that your people matter and their actions matter. The productivity that will be unleashed is likely to be nothing short of astonishing.

We have rarely witnessed more corporate leadership failures than we have over the past few years. Debacles in the financial industry, an oil spill in the Gulf, auto industry bankruptcies, and more have put corporate leaders on public display in an almost unprecedented way. And, for the most part, the ones who have failed so publicly have demonstrated, perhaps without intending to, that they have very little moral authority at all and few real values beyond making boatloads of money. Once trouble hits, these organizations are revealed to be among the most fragile and least able to respond nimbly. Their employees and customers simply don't care enough about the continued success of the company to do anything to help as it circles the drain—they may even be actively rooting for its demise. For every one of these failed or critically ill companies, when you look for any correlation between their stated values and their behaviors you will, almost always, find that there is none.

Companies that have significant misalignments between their values and their behavior are all too common, even when the consequences do not make headlines. A company may, for instance, claim to honor the value of cooperation and then set up compensation systems that encourage competition. By their actions and decisions, leaders create a culture, and culture always trumps any strategy you try to implement. To inspire top performance, your organization's strategy needs to be aligned with values that are meaningful for your customers and employees. Values need to be incorporated into the "operating instructions" of organizations—that is, into the day-to-day behaviors of its employees *and* its leaders. You can't just declare your values and hope that people will understand what to do with them. It is absolutely essential that you make values come alive for employees if you want them to change their behavior in ways that reflect those values. In other words, if you want to inspire employees to care about the company's performance, you must tie values and behavior to a few compelling metrics in the company and in their own teams. Simple scorecards showing how these metrics can be moved in response to individual effort are some of the most powerful tools in a leader's arsenal.

Unfortunately, most companies handle metrics by allowing only the leaders to see the important numbers. Concentrating everything in the hands of leaders gives them both too much control and too little ability to execute their strategies through the efforts of enthusiastic employees. Your employees need to see what the score is every week. They need to know how the company is doing, so that they can celebrate wins or help change things if they aren't working. The team and the individual need to know that *they*, not the boss, are responsible for beating the metrics. This is exactly what Ann Rhoades has been promoting for years.

I hope that Ann's book convinces leaders that the possibility of success lies in creating a shared vision in their people, based on values and reinforced by hiring, training, and rewards. As the economy recovers, it is time to get this message out so that companies can rebuild their businesses on a stronger foundation. In *Built on Values,* Ann Rhoades presents a systematic method for integrating values and values-based behavior into the daily life of everyone in the organization. Trust is the new leadership competency for the global economy, but trust cannot be forced. It must be earned.

Ann's model allows leaders to prove that they deserve that trust, by setting and upholding strong moral authority and inspiring values. Paradoxically, leaders gain authority and trust by giving authority away. The beauty of this book is that it shows exactly how to build a culture in which everyone (including the leader) feels listened to, respected, and valued. From the janitor to the executive suite, that's exactly what people need in order to perform beyond everyone's expectations.

INTRODUCTION: LAUNCHING A CULTURE CHANGE THE RIGHT WAY

It's not hard to understand why a company needs a culture that will encourage employees to treat customers well. Trouble is, nobody wants to tell you the "secret" of how to do that because then you might become a more formidable competitor. But I would like nothing better than to see a world filled with companies that have a positive, customer-oriented culture—so I'm going to let you in on those secrets and show you the exact steps for curing an ailing culture or creating a new one from scratch.

During my career I have been instrumental in helping create the high-performing cultures at some of the most admired companies in America: JetBlue, Southwest Airlines, Doubletree Hotels, P.F. Chang's China Bistros, Juniper Networks, Loma Linda University Medical Center, and many more. What I have learned from working with those companies is a simple truth: There is no "right" culture; there is only right fit. Defining the right fit is a process of determining what values are important to your organization's success and committing to them. You must then develop a plan for how people should behave based on those values and put it into practice throughout your organization. The most critical element, of course, is then helping your people adopt those behaviors and live those values, every day.

If you look at the behavior of leaders, you can tell what the values of a company really are. And all too often, those lived values bear almost no resemblance to the stated values—those painted on the walls or sanctified in a mission statement. Many leaders want to believe that all they need to do is proclaim a set of values and culture will magically change—but that does nothing to retool the actual values that control day-to-day actions on the front line. Changing those "inherent" values takes considerably more effort and cannot be accomplished by any leader or set of executives acting alone.

That is not to say that there is one true path to the best culture or even one best culture. I will not be recommending that you adopt a particular set of values. Far from it. "One size fits all" fits everyone poorly. A culture that works for you can only arise organically from the organization itself if it is going to fit with your leadership, values, products and, in particular, the desires of your customers and the aspirations of your employees. People Ink assists companies in identifying their underlying values and changing their cultures, but there is no reason why the people in your company cannot do it on their own.

If there is one secret shared by companies that create customer-centric cultures, it is that their leaders profoundly understand that people really are their biggest asset—and they act on that idea every day. Organizations that truly value people often don't use it as an advertising slogan. They just do it.

Throughout this book, I will be recommending that you involve front-line people in decisions and activities to a much greater extent than you may have experienced before. Keep an open mind about this. Trust that this is one of the secrets you really can steal from successful, high-spirit cultures.

There are many books describing the values and strategies that admired companies employ, but as many leaders have found to their distress, simply appropriating values-based programs wholesale from other companies doesn't really work. What no previous book has addressed in detail is the "how to" of building this kind of high-performing, sustainable culture based on shared values, and this book will fill that gap. *Built on Values* will show you:

- How to develop your own Values Blueprint and put it into action
- Why "living the values" is the first principle in leading people successfully
- How to exceed the expectations of employees and customers by living the values
- Why it's essential to hire, fire, and reward people based on values
- How to establish a discipline for sustaining a values-centric culture

Great cultures can't be replicated or copied; you must launch your own, based on values you and your people determine are best for your organization.

I remember laughing when reading an article on Richard Branson in 2009, in which he announced that Virgin America's new planes would be "equipped with mood lighting, Wi-Fi access, power outlets and touch screen entertainment networks at every seat. It's got to be twice as good as JetBlue," he said, "and a thousand times [better than] the rest." Sir Richard apparently believed that to be "twice as good" as JetBlue (and five hundred times better than every other airline, by implication), they only had to change the ambiance and technology offered with each seat. But in JetBlue's case it's not about the bells and whistles. It is always about the people: personal, sincere, warm people delivering great customer service. And Mr. Branson can't touch that with mood lighting.[1]

WHEN SHOULD YOU CONSIDER A CULTURE CHANGE?

When is a culture change necessary or appropriate? You should definitely consider it if (1) you are being outperformed in your category, (2) you have high turnover in key positions, (3) your employee and/or customer surveys are stubbornly low, or (4) if your financial performance is shaky or declining. More often than not, these issues are the result of an ailing culture, and by changing the culture you fix the problem. You should also consider a culture change if (5) you just want to go from good to great.

Built on Values and our Values Blueprint were developed from my experience with Southwest Airlines, JetBlue, Doubletree Hotels, P.F. Chang's, Loma Linda University Medical Center, and the many clients of People Ink. While working with these companies I have seen, over and over, that companies that put values-based cultures into place become higher performers, both in customer satisfaction *and* in financial return. At Loma Linda Medical Center, for instance, turnover was 30 percent per year before they went through the process of culture transformation. Not even a year into the change, turnover was down between 1 and 15 percent in every department, Even better, JetBlue and Southwest, which are examples of great cultures and emulate the model I describe in this book, are two of the few major airlines that showed positive balance sheets in the challenging economy.

Don't get me wrong. Most executives know what a great culture looks like. They are just unsure of how to implement one. It's a big job but one that is absolutely worthwhile.

When I give talks on the value of culture change to large groups of C-suite executives around the country, I always start out by asking a few simple questions:

- Where do you get the best customer service?
- Have you noticed that the very best companies in the world have the happiest employees?
- Which competitors do you have the hardest time hiring people away from?

Nordstrom's and Southwest are almost always in the top five answers to these questions. And in the cities where JetBlue flies, they're mentioned, too. Fly on Southwest and JetBlue and what will you hear the passengers say? They'll talk about what a pleasant experience it was and how things just seemed to be handled well, even when there were serious problems.

For example, in February 2007, when JetBlue was seven years old, an ice storm kept a plane full of passengers on the runway at JFK for ten hours. Just days after the incident, founder and CEO Dave Neeleman introduced a passenger's bill of rights, the first in the country, offering customers increasing levels of cash compensation based on the length of any flight delay that is the fault of JetBlue. They would get a $25 voucher for an hour of delay, a full fare for four hours or more. The document also promised that the company would find a way to get passengers off planes that had sat on the tarmac for five hours or more. (That full fare idea almost made it into the national Air Passengers' Bill of Rights, passed by Congress in April 2010. The airline industry fought it, though, so it was dropped from the final bill. In Europe, passengers' legal rights are already similar to JetBlue's.)

Even with the media storm that surrounded the incident, when we followed up with the passengers who had sat on the plane for ten hours, we found that 80 percent had a favorable opinion of JetBlue even after that horrible experience and were still flying the airline. Eighty percent. Most of them said it was because of JetBlue's honest and transparent response to the situation. In other words, JetBlue showed obvious remorse and committed to doing much better for them in the future. That's the kind of metric that makes the upheaval of culture change worthwhile.

BEGINNING THE PROCESS OF CHANGE

Your organization already has a culture, so you need to begin any change process by letting your people inform you about the culture that already exists. Once you have identified what your culture is, the next step is to identify the best culture to drive your organization's success. The ideal is a high-spirit culture where everyone is engaged for the good of the company. All the organizations included in this book have this kind of spirit, which comes from everyone steering in the same way, toward the same goals, with everyone helping everyone else. It is amazing how behavior changes and enthusiasm grows when values and culture are clear.

To make this work, involving your front-line people is essential. From the very beginning, the involvement of your best front-line people will begin to tie your culture more firmly to what is most important: giving customers such a satisfying experience that they will buy from you again and again. Front-line people, surrounded by customers every day, know how to do that. And the best ones are eager to tell you. Involving respected front-line people gives your culture change instant credibility.

From that initial process will emerge a Values Blueprint that codifies the values your people have agreed upon and the behaviors that exemplify those values. Values are only explicitly incorporated into daily operations by tying them to expected behaviors and rewarding your people for living them.

ATTRACT THE A PLAYERS

Elite employees, the best of the best—the A Players—are never begging for work. These people have jobs, even during an economic downturn. The best people typically never want for job offers but may have trouble finding a company where they are comfortable and happy. In fact, I believe that there is a rising "V-Generation," committed young workers who expect the places they work to reflect their own highest impulses. Your job is to create a culture where people want to work so you can attract the best talent.

The best players, no matter their age, look for companies whose values match their own and where they look forward to going to work every morning. But those rewarding and satisfying jobs are few and far between, even for them. In other words, you are looking for A Players, and they are, potentially, looking for a company like the one you aspire to create. In *Built on Values*, I lay out a method for changing your recruiting and hiring methods, so that you attract more than your share of A Players. My definition of A Players is somewhat different from some in academic circles. Quite simply, they are the people in your company whose skills and passions are well matched to their jobs, regardless of what their jobs may be. People who, through their behaviors, display the values of your organization daily. We are not just talking about recruiting A Players as leaders. In my experience in high-performing operations, I have found that A Players are needed *at every level* of the organization. At JetBlue and Southwest, baggage handlers take pride in the job they do and are obsessive about making sure the bags are handled carefully and without mistakes.

When you have the right hiring model, it is irrelevant whether or not it is a hirer's market. If you want to outperform the competition, you want the majority of your employees to be A Players. Your customers want that, too. Though they may not articulate or even realize why, customers want to do business more often with companies where the employees thrive in a culture that rewards the very best customer service.

Becoming a values-rich company is not necessarily going to make your search for A Players easier—you'll still interview a lot of people, at least at the HR level, while looking for top talent. But your definition of what "top talent" is will change as your ability to attract and retain them increases. You will find that more of your workforce comes from employee referrals, as current workers recommend people they know will fit into the culture because they understand it so well. You'll also attract a lot of attention from your competitors' A Players, who wonder what all the happiness is about at your place. And you will find them in completely unexpected places, because A Players are all around you once you stop to notice them.

One night in Dallas while my family was eating at Macaroni Grill, I was impressed by a waiter who offered fantastic, "over the top" service.

As I recall, he brought a complimentary dessert to our table because he thought we had waited too long for our food. With my encouragement, he came to interview at Southwest and was hired. He went on to recruit several fraternity brothers who exhibited the same service attributes. A number of those friends went on to serve as flight attendants for Southwest, after going through our rigorous values/behavior interviewing process.

That interviewing process, perhaps more so than any other piece of the Values Blueprint, will ensure that you select A Players. But all of the other components of your people and leadership processes also play a part in attracting and retaining a high proportion of A players in your organization. I will show you a way to integrate your values completely with your recruitment, hiring, training, compensation, performance metrics, rewards, communications, and even executive behavior.

SIX PRINCIPLES FOR CREATING A VALUES-RICH CULTURE

The Values Blueprint method of changing culture works. I have seen it happen over and over, in large companies and small, for-profits, non-profits, and every iteration in between. Single departments and work-groups can also use this to create islands of excellence, even if your leaders are not ready to buy in. Perhaps you can lead them to it though demonstrated results. Even though culture change will be driven by different values in every organization, six fundamental principles inform every successful values-based culture change.

- *Principle 1. You can't force culture. You can only create environment.* A culture is the culmination of the leadership, values, language, people processes, rules, and other conditions, good or bad, present within the organization. The organization's leaders are the most instrumental in creating the environment and provide the most direct influence on it.

However, they cannot "create culture," especially by assigning the task to a Culture Committee; they can only create the right conditions for it to arise. We certainly recommend that you set up such committees, but you must realize that neither they nor leaders themselves have complete control of what your culture will turn out to be. You can only create an environment that will help your desired culture emerge and flourish.

- *Principle 2: You are on the outside what you are on the inside . . . no debate.* What many leaders don't understand, except perhaps intellectually, is that you cannot create a great customer service organization if you treat employees badly. You can't force people to smile and treat customers well, especially when they feel ill-used themselves. Not surprisingly, those organizations that do customer service best also treat their employees best. The bottom line? The service you provide for your customers will *never* be greater than the service you provide to your employees.

- *Principle 3: Success is doing the right things the right way.* One of the best reasons for redefining corporate values is that they can help us make better decisions. And the front line is where most decisions about customer service should be made. In a company where customer service is one of the values, one of the behaviors tied to it could be empowering front-line people with tools and knowledge to handle problems personally and immediately. A win there is a happy customer who did not have to speak to a supervisor. By defining your values and the behaviors based on them, you also simplify the task of day-to-day decision making: "Does that make sense in light of our values?" is all you have to ask.

- *Principle 4: People do exactly what they are incented to do.* At one large manufacturer of mobility equipment, an incentive paid more for faster deliveries. The result might seem predictable to anyone outside the company: Aggressive delivery people almost literally tossed the equipment off trucks at elderly customers so they could rush off to the next one. This is probably not the behavior the company wanted to induce, even though it is the result they incented. The model of culture I will show you, however, requires rewarding the behaviors you do want, taking into account how they lead to an outcome. This is made easier with simple values-based performance metrics. In addition, your values will be perceived as hollow and meaningless unless you base compensation and rewards on expressions of the behaviors that go along with the values. Hiring and performance appraisal methods, too, must be revised to select people who already display the values important to you. And you must be courageous enough to fire those who don't. Even long-time employees. Even executives. Otherwise, they will render your ideal culture impossible.

- *Principle 5: Input = Output.* Organizations will only get out of something what they are willing to put into it. Values maintenance—what we call continuous improvement—is as important as values creation. In other words, you are never fully "done" with culture; you must be always vigilant that no one backslides into old ways. This requires regular monitoring of progress toward full implementation of the model, as well as values-based leadership development and succession planning.
- *Principle 6: The environment you want can be built on shared, strategic values and financial responsibility.* Conscious action, beginning with determining a set of shared values, can set up the necessary condition for encouraging a culture that will make an organization into a leader in its industry. It should almost go without saying that those values should also be vetted in terms of responsible fiscal management. Happy-talk values that result in spending huge sums of money on questionable programs are not values that are sustainable in the long run. But neither should you let financial concerns derail the process in its infancy. Counsel your financial people to give it a chance—it is likely to save buckets of money sooner rather than later as turnover and training costs go down. It can even help companies avoid the high cost of layoffs—which will no longer be a first resort to cut costs—that have been shown to hurt stock price anyway as investors flee from a troubled company.[2] Values are most critical when making tough decisions, but that is also when they come in handiest to illuminate the way forward.

WHO NEEDS VALUES?

All companies need a values culture in order to attract the best people and compete effectively. People coming out of college today are looking for a company that reflects their values. The case can be made that companies who are the best in their categories, like JetBlue and Southwest, consciously create cultures that make that success possible. And those cultures are based on positive values but are defined by and are unique to each organization. There is no such thing as one-size-fits-all values.

All leaders will benefit from the step-by-step instructions in this book that will help create such a culture, whether they're a CEO, a board member, or a front-line team leader and whether they're trying to shift the attitudes of the executive team or the front-line employees. In fact, the attitudes of your executive team members are just as important as employee attitudes if you want to become a company with strong, profit-enhancing values. If the behavior of your executives does not reflect the values that your company supposedly values, no one will believe that values are important. If one of your values is "caring," but you let a senior manager yell at employees, everyone will know that caring carries no weight in your organization. This is especially true of the CEO, who should always be aware that every little thing a CEO does or does not do is noticed by those lower down the ladder.

All across the country, my team is helping companies use values and their associated behaviors to deliver on their brand promises, create new brand personalities, and make execution of corporate strategies less of a Herculean struggle. Defined and agreed-upon behaviors from the bottom of the company to the top afford considerable flexibility in crafting responses to competitive pressures and make the organization more responsive and nimbler. After all, if you can count on employees to help you carry out your mission rather than grumbling, you'll have an unstoppable team on your hands.

At JetBlue, we knew we wanted to create exactly that type of culture when we in the executive team sat down to create our brand-new airline. Over several days of brainstorming, we identified five values we personally wanted to experience in an airline: safety, integrity, caring, passion, and fun. We put those values in place; we celebrated them every day; we hired people who shared those values; and we set up systems to recognize employees who were living those values. It was as simple—and as complex—as that.

The key is to focus on both the big picture and the smallest detail at the same time. It sounds difficult, like spinning a couple of hundred plates in the air at the same time. But it really isn't, when leaders realize that everything they do and everything they say can either reinforce or destroy their efforts to change their culture. *Built on Values* is based on that very simple principle. Changing a culture starts with getting the basics right (values and behavior at the C-level). Then the big things (hiring the right people, keeping them, and delighting customers) fall more easily into place.

The big question is how to implement something like this in practice. After my speeches, there are always some executives who come up to me afterwards and want to know how to get started right now, today. They ask for copies of my slides and detailed information about the Values Blueprint. What they all say, fundamentally, is, "We really need to do this, but no one has ever told us how. It sounds like things would actually get easier once we put your system into place." They are absolutely right about that.

Built on Values provides a clear road map for how to accomplish culture change, not just inspirational stories of great cultures. This is a model that I have used for twenty-five years, and it has worked for companies in many industries: health care, IT, retail, services, financial, and more. If you take the steps I recommend to implement the Values Blueprint, you will find a simple path to a great culture. Complexity and extraneous work tend to fall away once your employees understand which values are truly fundamental, because the behaviors associated with those values are always rewarded. It becomes easy for them to see what they should be doing with each moment of their time. Going a step further, if it becomes plainly apparent to everyone that their leaders are in the trenches with them, working as hard for a common goal, culture change isn't that hard at all.

CHAPTER 1

IS A VALUES-BASED CULTURE WORTH THE EFFORT?

A high-performing culture doesn't just happen. It can't be forced into being through willpower. But it can become an inevitability if you create the right environment to foster it. We have found that to move to a positive, performance-enhancing culture, leaders simply need to model the values and behaviors they want to see in employees *and* create systems to reinforce those behaviors. Yes, it is simple conceptually. You can change culture by design if you remember that you can influence how your employees think. Your corporate culture can actually elicit cooperation and commitment from employees, almost without their awareness, if your values are clear and your systems are properly designed to reinforce them. And, perhaps surprisingly, a strong corporate culture can have a huge and direct impact on performance.

In the course of my work, I have become convinced that positive, people-centered corporate values lead to higher performance. Perhaps you have noticed that in the thirty-five years of its values-rich existence, Southwest Airlines is the only airline that has been profitable during every one of those years. Research similarly supports these findings. For example, Harvard professor Rosabeth Moss Kanter studied large market leaders worldwide that she calls "vanguard companies." She has found that these companies have been able to nimbly deal with challenges and transform themselves when necessary because they are "fundamentally driven by a core set of values."[1] A 2008 American Management Association study found that a "positive corporate culture" is associated with higher performance.[2] And as far back as 1999, Ronald Burt suggested that a good culture was a "competitive asset associated with economic performance." Burt, a professor of Sociology and Strategy at the University of Chicago Booth School of Business, found that almost 25 percent of the return in his sample companies was accounted for by the relative strength of their corporate culture.[3] More recently, a study of thirty large corporations over the past five years by consulting firm Senn Delany in Los Angeles showed that culture change "led from the top and encompassing every part of the organization can deliver huge cost savings, improve performance, and boost profitability."[4]

Too many leaders, though, feel that corporate culture is a low priority, especially when compared to running the business day-to-day. My colleagues in culture-rich companies would respectfully disagree. "The best companies—those with clearly articulated values and a sense of direction—have a constant sense of urgency but they're not frantic and under enormous stress," noted Joel Peterson, chairman of the board of JetBlue, founder and chairman of Peterson Partners, and former CEO, Trammell Crow. Is your company like an emergency room, he asks, a survival culture that's just trying to keep the company alive or maximize sales or new product development? That works great for a while, but your best people will burn out eventually. Remember, the best employees—your A Players—have options, no matter what the economy is like. In the war for talent, as in the war for profit, culture does make a difference.[5]

DOES YOUR COMPANY NEED A CULTURE CHANGE?

If your turnover is high, your customers are unhappy, and your A Players can't wait to leave, you need a culture change. In a business that needs culture change, the best employees—the A Players—don't have any loyalty to your company. They know they can command good pay and good working conditions anywhere. So when rough times hit, many just hunker down, confident that a better opportunity will come along eventually. They'll run when it does. The B and C players may be running, too. High turnover, in fact, is a waving red flag that culture change is necessary.

You may even need a culture adjustment if your company or division is doing pretty well. You may be making your goals. But if your employees don't understand your company's values—and what behaviors exemplify those values—then you are missing an opportunity to achieve greater success. In those circumstances, those results you may be proud of today won't last. You'll plug along; long-term performance will never approach greatness. Worse, without solid, behavior-based values, you are vulnerable to employee poaching by any competitor who discovers how to define and live up to values that employees can be proud of.

When a culture isn't working as well as it should for an organization, it shouldn't come as a shock to its leaders, but it often does. One client I worked with spent two years avoiding speaking one-on-one with his people and ignoring feedback as he struggled to keep the company out of bankruptcy. He thought he still had a great relationship with the rank and file because every time he gave a speech, he emphasized the positives of the situation. Strangely, his people told us that they were telling him all along that the culture was fragmenting under the strain, but he swears that he hadn't heard them say anything was wrong.

One of the values that developed in his company, obviously, was the need to protect the CEO from bad news. His employees felt sorry for him, struggling as he was under the strain, so they decided to keep him in the dark. Clearly he needed a culture change. We helped him figure out, with the input of his people, that two important values this company needed to adopt were transparency and humility. The first step this leader took after that was to immediately go out and tour every one of his facilities. He told his employees about the turnaround that he was still in the midst of and (very difficult for him) asked for assistance. Even with two years of miscommunication to recover from, most employees decided to pitch in and help.

We all know the names of companies that have run into problems because of negative cultures or cultures not focused on customers—for instance, airlines that started charging for bags during hard economic times. JetBlue has not considered charging for baggage because doing so simply does not fit in with its of value of caring, both for employees and customers. Although the company may make more money on a baggage charge, employees take the brunt of negative customer feedback. Huge financial gains could result in the short term, but there could be real consequences down the road as customers move to other carriers who do not charge those fees. Caring about customers is simply too important a value for JetBlue and Southwest to trample on it with something as trivial as bag charges, even though doing so could afford them large short-term financial gains.

Does your company need a culture change? Or does it just need to tie employee behaviors to its perfectly fine values? Most companies could improve in both areas. Others are in need of a radical values overhaul. Where your company falls on the continuum doesn't matter, really. It has been our experience that every company that decides to embark on the Values Blueprint process will see some improvement in these areas:

- *People problems.* Turnover rates higher than your industry are a red flag, as are concerted efforts to unionize. In addition, employee satisfaction surveys that are screaming with either dissatisfaction or indifference are often ignored or not action-planned against for too long.
- *Customer satisfaction.* If your company has not defined good customer service behaviors, customers will suffer, as will repeat business and profits. Once you begin to understand values-oriented behavior, you will see examples of the *lack* of it all around you. How prevalent is it in your company?

- *Falling quality scores.* Quality lags first become apparent in many companies in a growing problem with cleanliness and order. Are your employee restrooms a mess? Do your people litter your grounds or allow debris to accumulate in their work areas? In this situation, quality control will soon start identifying growing numbers of preventable errors.
- *Lack of trust.* If leaders are not transparent and straightforward, that is a value that will quickly spread throughout the organization. Leaders who repeatedly lie about provable things, like performance results, are showing what the organization values through their actions.

The Bernie Madoffs and Enrons of the world had a skin-deep attitude toward values that worked fine until, suddenly, it was exposed as a fraud. These companies were among those that professed to take values the most seriously. They just didn't live the values that they put on the wall. They had values all right, but they were the unspoken ones: greed and hunger for power.

CULTURE BY DESIGN

Obviously, I think creating a culture on purpose is far superior to just letting your culture grow without guidance (which it will). But I am not proposing that companies adopt some ideal set of values that can somehow magically create a high-performing culture. No such set of ideal values exists, although caring, integrity, customer focus, and the like routinely appear in the Values Blueprints I help companies create. Rather, the values that are right for your company depend on your competitive space, your product offerings, your target customers, and many other factors unique to your company.

As I'll discuss in detail in upcoming chapters, your goal in the design phase of the culture change process is to develop a set of values and value-based behaviors that everyone in your company can embrace. Written down and summarized in a one-page document, this is what I call a Values Blueprint. The first step in implementing a Blueprint that works for you is to figure out what set of values operates in your company now. It is essential to assess what value systems your employees at all levels believe they are operating under as well as their behaviors when faced with important decisions. It is necessary to delve deeply into exactly how employees and customers feel about the company and its values in order to know where changes in those values are necessary. The more information you collect at this point on the "is state" of the company, the better your ability to construct a new set of values that will capitalize on your strengths and create a high-functioning company for your customers. Themes and trends will emerge from your assessment process that will be essential to an understanding of the values and behaviors that will fit your company and its goals.

The next step in the process is naming a Values Committee (five to thirty people, depending on the size of the company) that will be in charge of the overall process of change. These employees should be drawn from all areas of the company, especially from top-performing, committed employees on the front line. Unless you involve such employees, the process will have little credibility and is very likely to fail. After this step, it won't take long to embark on real change. Your Values Committee will go off-site for a two-day Values Workout retreat and will use the assessment data collected, as well as their own knowledge, to hammer out a preliminary set of values and behaviors. What they bring back—a draft Values Blueprint—is then subject to discussion and vetting throughout the company, not just in the executive suite. Most of my clients find that, if they've listened to the assessment piece and included front-line employees in the process, they get more praise than criticism for the values and behaviors they come home with.

And then the essential piece: the Values Blueprint needs to be tightly integrated into your organization's DNA and used for every subsequent decision in the organization, including hiring, compensation, benefits, communications, and even executive behavior. If it isn't, you might as well just hang it up on the wall and forget about it.

HIRING BY DESIGN

Not every talented person will thrive in every company culture. You need to create a system of hiring whereby you hire people who share your organization's values. Just hiring the most talented and experienced person does not mean you're hiring the best person for your company. In fact, David Neeleman, the founder of JetBlue, would probably admit that he didn't quite fit with the culture when he worked at Southwest. He was constantly questioning how things were done there, pushing people to upgrade technology, and generally questioning twenty years of success. (I know; I was there.) "What to do about David" became a topic of constant discussion. David eventually went on to found West Jet in Canada and eventually JetBlue and developed cultures that were much more in line with his thinking regarding technology. He is the father of the e-ticket, after all.

Unlike David, other people will simply keep their heads down so they can keep collecting a paycheck. Meanwhile, you are filling your organization with employees who just aren't happy or excited about their work. Some of the best companies recognize this dilemma and deal with it directly. Zappos.com offers new hires $2,000 to quit within ninety days after training if the new employees don't think they are a match for the Zappos corporate culture.[6]

What if your organization is already full of people simply biding their time and collecting a paycheck? Some kind of mismatch of environment and culture is obviously going on, but it is often not clear what it is. Are you hiring the wrong people? Why is that? In many cases, the "wrong" people are hired because line managers are not at all sure how to hire people to fit into the corporate culture. Your company's values may simply be words on a wall or in print that are ignored in practice.

Managers probably don't even know what specific behaviors to look for in employee interviews so that new hires will fit into your existing culture. Maybe your culture itself is the problem: in the struggle for growth and profit, it may have grown up without much conscious thought devoted to the behaviors that will contribute to long-term success. Your culture may now be something that actually makes it harder for your company to be successful.

If no one articulates what the real values of the company are, managers are left to glean them from the CEO's speeches and actions, memos from corporate, and their own performance reviews. And glean they will. As a result, in a lot of companies, managers might as well be reading tea leaves or putting fingers up in the wind to see in which direction they should tack. So is it any surprise that hiring managers fall back on the old reliable standards of hiring people they like, whose resumes look presentable, and hoping for the best? Not surprisingly, that sort of hit-or-miss hiring method results in a lot of misfires. If you have never really thought about (or been told) what your company values, you just cross your fingers and hope that your new hires will "fit in."

Len Trainor, CEO of the thousand-employee Heritage Home Health Care, tells the story of a woman he would definitely have hired before the company went through the Values Blueprint process that I recommend in this book. After her interview, Trainor says, his reaction was "I like her—we hit it off." But he also recalled, "She rambled a lot and couldn't give a complete story of handling a crisis with a patient from start to finish. It was obvious the situation was never resolved to the satisfaction of the patient, and we didn't hire her. But we would have in the past because I liked her so much, personally."[7] I would have loved to have known about this method in the early days of my own career. When I was the HR and marketing officer for a bank, the first person I hired was a head teller. I chose her because I thought she was a nice person and she had prior experience. The next day, she walked out of the bank with the entire coin vault wrapped as Christmas presents. Moral to the story: there is more to hiring than "gut feel." Should

I have been interviewing for the values of integrity and honesty? You bet. But the company's priority was to find someone experienced to fill the position—and do it in a hurry. With some better interviewing methods (which I'll be showing you in detail later), I might have realized that what this woman did not value was honesty.

In a values-based interview, for example, you wouldn't ask people to tell you their strengths and weaknesses; you'd ask them to tell a story. We advise hospital clients, for example, to include a question about how prospective employees saved a life or changed an outcome for the better by telling the truth to superiors, regardless of consequences. If one of your values is integrity and the prospective employee can't think of an example in which she told the truth even when her job was at risk, she's probably not a good match. I wish I had known to ask that when I was hiring the head teller!

A BLUEPRINT FOR VALUES

Loma Linda University Medical Center, based in California, is a century-old institution that, with some effort, got the culture, the hiring, and the entire blueprint for a values driven organization exactly right. Loma Linda has always had a great reputation in the community; however, in 2006 actual patient satisfaction after a stay was only 42 percent in the Gallup Organization survey. "We wanted to move from good to great," notes Dr. Gerald Winslow, vice president of mission and culture at Loma Linda. "You can teach people best practices, but that doesn't mean they will actually do them unless they are reinforced."[8] In that, they are succeeding spectacularly well—by 2009 Gallup patient-satisfaction scores had risen to 86 percent and continue to rise.

Loma Linda began the process as all of our clients do, by naming a permanent Values Committee made up of people from all areas of the hospital, including front-line employees, doctors, nurses, support staff, and a couple of people from top management. They spent two days clarifying their values and working on the Blueprint: they felt, because of their reputation with prospective patients, that their core values were good. Teamwork, wholeness, integrity, compassion, and excellence were the values that emerged from this process. (Conveniently, they formed the acronym TWICE, now often used to remind employees to think twice about values.)

This is where many culture change efforts end. Slap those values up on the wall and expect everyone to figure out for themselves how to live them.

In order to make sure the values were, instead, percolated through the entire organization, Loma Linda embarked on an effort to tie values to specific behaviors, in every job category. Teams of hiring managers and A Players in each department, selected by the Values Committee, identified the key attributes for each and every job and tied them to one of the values. The work of these teams allowed the hospital group to create an interview guide for each position that not only verified the attributes but also identified a cultural match.

Then the hospital group implemented a new copyrighted leadership model called SOAR (Select, Orient, Appraise, Recognize) to make sure that values-based behavior was selected for and reinforced at all levels. The first step, "Select," begins with teaching managers values-based hiring techniques at an all-day seminar. Temporary workers were hired and brought in to serve as interviewees during live practice sessions. "It was a revelation to me and the other leaders," notes Winslow. "We discovered that we didn't do interviewing particularly well when it comes to hiring for our values, but there was still some resistance because they felt they already knew how to interview."

Loma Linda also had A Players from the staff level participate in the training and demonstrate the interview techniques. Winslow called that "truly revolutionary" because the A Players pick up on things leaders don't. "Instead of 'tell me about yourself,' you'll hear the A Players ask things like 'tell me what you did when you had a really unreasonable deadline to cope with,'" says Winslow. "And what you don't hear in the answers is 'typically' or 'generally' or 'we,' at least from the people you want to hire. You find a lot of enthusiasm in people who relate to the values and a lot of eye contact. We look for that."

Another innovation for Loma Linda is the selection team. Three people, a manager, an A Player peer, and an HR staffer interview each prospective hire. And any one of them can be overruled by the other two. "Did you ever stop to think how much more time people spend choosing a copy machine than a colleague?" asked Winslow. "How much more time does it take to fix a mistaken hire?"

Once the hiring decision is made, the next vital step at Loma Linda is "Orientation and Onboarding." Winslow says that orientation formerly consisted of "laying out rules in a fairly perfunctory and mind-numbing way." (Sound familiar?) The hospital group now calls orientation "Living Our Values Day" and tries to make it fun and participatory. The day is hosted by the CEO or a senior VP, and much of the first day is spent discussing stories about our values and letting employees talk about their values. And rather than presenting a lecture about employee benefits, the leaders take new hires on a tour of things like the fitness center, which Winslow calls their "benefits fair." The more boring elements, required by compliance, are livened up with a team-based quiz show and generous prizes for knowledge. And at the end of the day, new employees are asked to fill out a personal commitment card. This will be opened in ninety days by the employee and a supervisor together. "The purpose is to provide the employee an opportunity to reflect on the values they expect to be living by from now on," says Winslow.

After you've hired the right people, the most important thing you can do is make them want to perform at a top level—the A level. Your people will follow you off a cliff if you have set up systems and "Appraisals"—the third element of SOAR—that provide them with rewards for values-based behavior. And they'll do what's necessary to mirror those behaviors, almost without effort, because they have the comfort level of knowing what's expected and being rewarded for it.

The result? Turnover decreases, sometimes dramatically, satisfaction goes up all around, and financial metrics show positive movement.

At Loma Linda, the interview guide has been incorporated into a computerized multi-rater evaluation system. Each employee is evaluated by three peer raters, their manager, and themselves. About 50 percent of the weight is given to living the values and meeting goals; the rest is given to specific job performance criteria that constitute a "mirror image" of the interview process. "It is laughable now that before we started this process, we were giving 5 percent weight to meeting goals," says Winslow. "I expected a lot of pushback on that, but I got very little. People want to work on a good team and be evaluated on behaviors that are not subjective."

The final piece at Loma Linda, and in similar form for all of my clients, is "Recognize." If you don't reward people (and not just with money) for exhibiting the values, they will assume the program is just more management hot air. You must also remember that not everyone wants to be recognized in the same way.

I've found that you don't even need huge monetary rewards if employees feel the leaders appreciate what they are doing. JetBlue's founding CEO Dave Neeleman and then-president Dave Barger (now CEO) sent personal thank-you notes and also regularly published company-wide "Blue Notes" to recognize great behavior. At Southwest, to my amazement, CEO Herb Kelleher of Southwest kept track of eight thousand employee collections and tried to send a new piece to employees he wanted to recognize: a signed baseball, say, or a Hummel figurine—whatever the employee collected. But even that would not have come close to creating JetBlue's and Southwest's high-functioning customer-oriented culture if those leadership actions had not been based on clear values tied to desired behaviors. You must first clearly delineate the behavior you want before you can elicit those behaviors and extinguish others. And it is essential that those behaviors are directly derived from the values you determine are important for success.

LEADERS DRIVE CULTURE

Think about how your people would react if they were asked to step up and help the company thrive—or even survive. Would they sign on for shared sacrifice? Or would they look at your salary and perks and say, "You first"? Would they remember that you hardly ever visit them and talk to them personally? Or would they recall the many ways you've helped out personally when things got rough?

In 2008, Dave Barger, the CEO of JetBlue, took a 50 percent pay cut. He did that so that no layoffs or pay cuts would have to reach employees when jet fuel prices headed for the stratosphere. That's the kind of thing that employees remember. But it also helped the airline weather the horrible travel year of 2009. According to Standard and Poor's, JetBlue experienced the only positive returns in the airline industry, recording $3.4 billion in revenues, a 19.2 percent increase over the previous year. At Starbucks, which also experienced challenges beginning in 2006, chairman Howard Schultz was famous for visiting shops all over the world to talk to employees about their experiences and mix a frappé or two. Schultz stepped back into the role of Starbucks CEO in 2008 after a hiatus of eight years, and in fiscal year 2009 income grew 23.9 percent, although as of this writing they haven't completely come back to pre-recession levels.[9] Is this recovery the result of Schultz's making an effort to reach out to employees? I think it definitely has to do with his intense focus on people. It says something when a CEO closes nine hundred stores at the same time in order to spend three hours retraining employees.

When you are a leader of a company, division, or department, every one of your actions matters, but particularly those that display your true values. Your people talk about everything you do, and it becomes a part of your company's DNA. The best leaders understand the incredible impact their actions have on how employees behave every day. I've worked closely with more than my share of leaders who were acutely aware of everything they did and used it consciously to shape their corporate cultures. But it was never so plain to me as it was one day shortly after I joined Doubletree Hotels. When Rick Kelleher, the CEO, and I travelled to one of the major cities within the Doubletree system, the regional manager of Doubletree in that city decided to send a limo to pick us up. Then Rick told him to "cancel the limo" because he felt it would make us look elitist to the employees who would be greeting us. To him, it was all about servant leadership, and he knew that the "optics" of any given situation are what people remember.

Think twice about the Porsche and the private jet, too. Employees who feel that their leadership team is flaunting their status will be significantly less motivated to make any extra effort for your company's success. Changing your culture from "my company" to "our company," on the other hand, will make a big difference.

THE CIRCLE OF EXCELLENCE

Great leaders are driven by competitiveness and performance. They want success for themselves—and for the people they lead. They understand that long-term success is possible only when you inspire the people around you to come to work every day prepared to do their best. Those are the leaders whose employees will do their very best for the company in good times and bad.

This is what you must drive home to your people—they are in charge of moving your company to a new "wow state." In a very real sense, all of your employees must become leaders who are responsible for executing the values your company will live by going forward. But here's the real slap upside the head: if your values are inspiring and connected to behaviors, hiring, and rewards, *your culture will become higher performing by itself.* You'll be creating a self-reinforcing circle of excellence that will operate even when you're not looking, because you are selecting for the behaviors you want, then rewarding those behaviors. People will do what they are incented to do, every time.

Your senior leaders also play a vital role in creating a self-reinforcing culture of excellence. Figure 1.1 shows how.

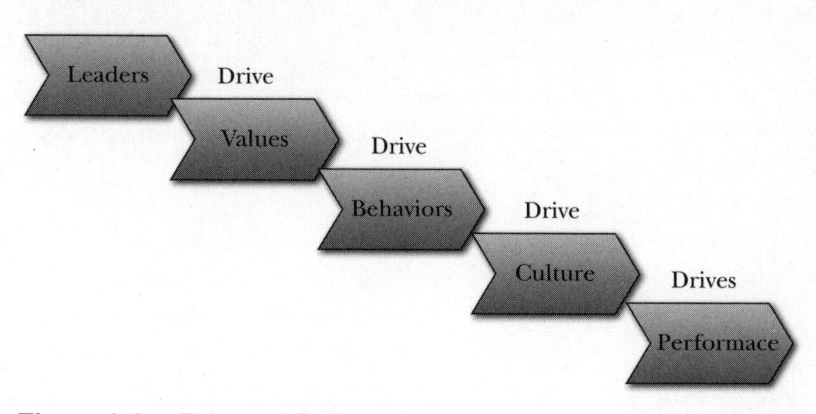

Figure 1.1. Drivers of Performance

- *Leaders drive values* by making the commitment to a values-based culture and leading by example.
- *Values drive behaviors* by acting as a mechanism for illustrating to employees what acceptable behavior in the company looks like. Values must be defined by behaviors that any employee can recognize and emulate.
- *Behaviors drive culture* because the collective behaviors of people in the organization are, by definition, the culture, for good or ill. Leaders must create the environment that encourages a high-performance culture based on values.
- *Culture drives performance* because people who are committed to and understand the values and behaviors will take responsibility for performance.

To ensure that you are hiring and retaining the right people, who will behave in ways that make your company succeed, you need to make sure that values and behaviors reinforce each other, from the top of the company to the bottom. The challenge is determining what your values are, whether they need changing, and what behaviors you want to reinforce.

CHAPTER 2

"SO HOW'S THAT WORKING FOR YOU?"

Uncover Your Company's True Values

Many leaders start with a belief that their organizations have already identified their values. Maybe they have. However, if you identified values years ago, but never really acted on them or made them part of your company's DNA, you cannot assume they are still relevant to the current needs of your organization. Could the random employee in the hall give you a coherent answer if you asked what the company's values are?

Even if you think values are unimportant or don't acknowledge them at all, your company's values and culture are actively attracting customers or driving them away. The best people are either knocking down your door or running for the exits. Your employees are either innovative and productive or just getting through the day. I often talk to business executives who tell me that they are having business problems but cannot believe these are related to culture. In their minds, culture is simply not a factor in business results, so they ignore it. "So how's that working for you?" I'll ask. I'll then have them consider their latest results from employee satisfaction surveys, customer feedback, turnover, critical incidents, and financial results, and in light of all those factors they often reconsider their answer. "Not very well," it turns out.

Consider it an iron law of business: Culture develops, regardless of whether or not it is defined. And if the values you've formally written down don't match the existing culture, those values will be ignored. Employees instinctively understand the unwritten rules of "how things really work around here." Most of them, especially the A Players, know exactly how to behave in order to stay employed until the day they walk out the door for something better. And they know what your company values, without being told. They understand the environment in which they are expected to thrive, even if it doesn't match their values and behaviors. So never make the mistake of thinking you'll be starting from a blank slate when you decide to pursue culture change, except when you are starting a brand-new company. However, the experience of many companies has shown that you can definitely shape your culture in ways that make it a more effective driver of business success—or failure.[1]

"If your culture doesn't reflect what people think about and spend their time on, you have a sick culture," notes JetBlue chairman Joel Peterson, who is also a lecturer on leadership and entrepreneurship at Stanford. "One of my entrepreneurship students, who already had his own business and was busy growing it, said, 'I don't need a culture in my business—we're growing fine.' And my students (I was so proud of them) said, 'You already have a culture, one that reflects your disdain for your culture and your people.' He had to agree that what they were saying was true."[2]

We were very lucky at JetBlue that we were able to consciously create a culture from scratch. We sat in a room—there were only ten of us at the time—and asked, "What do we want JetBlue to do and what do we want to stand for?" We wanted a set of values through which we could consider every decision. So we said, "Let's not put a huge mission statement on the wall, something that no one, including ourselves, is ever going to be able to repeat. Let's have something unique but very simple." We decided to build values around "bringing humanity back to air travel." The best values are simple values, and you should have no more than five to seven, or people will not remember them. They are the way you get back to Business 101; they are the basic outline of what your company is about. If you create your values correctly, it won't look complicated. It never does at high-performing organizations. If organizations are built around values and behaviors that support those values, employees behave the right way almost automatically. Flight attendants who have bought into "fun" as a value and really believe in it are relaxed and playful with customers every day without thinking about it. Employees in these companies behave in a way that is consistent with the company's values almost without exception. And they do it on a continuing basis, day after day after day.

As a result of going through that process at several companies, I began to recognize that you can, in fact, create a model where you can energize people every day, and you can make it happen in all kinds of environments. At JetBlue, we wanted employees to always deliver a remarkable experience for customers and great results for the company. But we also understood—and this is critical—that we could not make "financial success" a value to hang a company on. Instead, by discovering values that fit the company, and using those values to attract people whose behaviors reflect them, your company will allow a passion for success to emerge among your employees. Rather than being a value, financial success is actually a goal to aim for as you go through the process of consciously setting your values and creating a values blueprint.

As Herb Kelleher of Southwest says all the time, "Culture is what people do when no one is looking." If you fly Southwest, you know exactly what kind of service you will receive. I believe that Southwest is able to underpromise and overdeliver on its service because it has confidence that thirty thousand–plus people will do things consistently well every day. Jackie and Kevin Freiburg, former Southwest employees and authors of *Nuts! Southwest Airlines' Crazy Recipe for Business and Personal Success,* define that kind of culture as "the glue that holds our organizations together. It encompasses beliefs, norms, rituals, communication patterns, symbols, heroes and reward structures. Culture is not about magic formulas and secret plans; it is a combination of a thousand things."[3]

Every culture is different, of course, and what works for someone else may fall flat for you. The Southwest Airlines culture may not fly in your organization, but successful companies across the spectrum of industries make variations of Southwest's caring, focused culture work for them. That culture also recognizes that while business is deadly serious, fun can be a productive part of the culture. Any culture that respects its people and customers can create and maintain a long-term competitive advantage by doing what it does better than any competitors. The most important question is whether you are using your culture purposefully to enhance your chances for success.

Culture is your bedrock. It is how you will make decisions and how people in your company will view the world. And if you have a purposeful culture, you will be able to make good business decisions that seem, on their face at least, to be counterintuitive. Okay, they look crazy. One of the directors of Starbucks once told me the story of how they decided whether their restaurants in Japan would be nonsmoking. When they were making the decision, chairman Howard Schultz held a board meeting and talked about how everyone smoked in Japan. He was very concerned, as were others, that if they did not allow smoking, the Starbucks units in the country would fail or not get a good return on their investment. So he went around the room and asked each director to make a decision on whether they should allow smoking. He said that he would like everyone to look at the values and look at what we stand for before you make your decision, even knowing the cost of entry to the market is extremely high. They all said that one of things we believe in is protecting the environment and, because of that, that all previous units have been nonsmoking.[4] The result was that they did very well providing a nonsmoking environment in Japan because it turned out that a lot of Japanese people appreciated having a place to get away from smoke. So they lived their values and were financially successful. It was a difficult decision for them because the investment cost was incredibly high to get into Japan. Yet Starbucks discovered that living your values consistently—and using them to make hard decisions—resulted in a great outcome.

Conscious cultures don't always result in good decision making, however. It is important to define your culture but also to make sure you constantly monitor it for its ability to generate good outcomes. So is your culture a good one that needs tweaking or a dud? Trust me, you won't know for sure until you perform an assessment of your culture gap. To establish a blueprint for change, you have to understand the current state of the culture and the effectiveness of systems you already have in place. With that information in hand, leadership can then identify the desired outcomes and plan steps for change. Changing culture is really no different than retooling a plant, except that the tools are people and systems rather than people and machinery.

THE CULTURE GAP: MEASURING YOUR CURRENT CULTURE

Before you can hope to change your culture, you must begin with an objective sense of its current state of function or dysfunction. Assessing the "is state" of a culture can be one of the most mentally challenging tasks of the whole blueprint process because you are so close to it and so emotionally invested. Your natural tendency will be to protest, as the data begins rolling in, "No, wait, that's not the way things are here." Resisting that natural impulse is essential. We've seen it time and again among our clients. Leaders everywhere suffer from the completely understandable notion that because "people are our most important asset" or because the economy is weak, employees really are all giddily happy to be employed at their company, and their customers love them to death, too. Leaders are often in for a shock when they read the survey results, especially in cultures where hiding bad news from executives is the norm.

Culture cannot be interrogated directly, however. "Asking employees to describe their corporate culture is akin to asking a fish to describe what water is like," say Chris Edmonds and Bob Glaser, senior consulting managers for The Ken Blanchard Companies. "Neither the employee nor the fish can do it properly because they are both immersed in it."[5] Dispassionate analysis, though, is absolutely critical when it comes to assessing your current culture and systems. Leaders who feel it will be difficult to be objective should think about hiring outside researchers to perform the gap analysis I am about to recommend. This is especially the case if you fear that the trust level is low in your organization. And some organizations, like health care companies, are required to validate any surveys that they do, so they may want to hire a consultant or use free online resources to do this. There is something to be said for having an external entity to point to if results are not as positive as you might have liked. You wouldn't be doing this if you didn't think that the culture in your organization could use improvement, but that doesn't make negative feedback any easier to take.

I have found that outcomes are most reliable when you rely on four distinct sources of information for your values assessment: existing data, custom anonymous surveys, one-on-one interviews, and focus groups. With all of these methods, you are attempting to assess the values your employees display in everyday interactions, their feelings about your current systems, how knowledgeable they are about your current business model, and the level of trust in the organization. But doing so is not always as straightforward as it sounds. Many employees—and management—may be fearful that the information gathering will adversely affect their jobs or eliminate them. Others will be disdainful of what they perceive as yet another initiative that will only delay or disrupt their "real work."

Therefore the essential first step in the assessment process does not involve assessment at all. This is the time to lay your cards on the table and talk about exactly what you are up to.

Action Step 1: Fanfare!

Communicate to everyone in the company that you are beginning a journey to refine the company's values and make this a better place to work. You need to be absolutely transparent and lay out a strong case for the change that is necessary in your corporate culture. Use vivid stories about stellar work being done in your company (name names) as well as some of the serious problems that have caused you to take this action. Talk about metrics like profitability and turnover. A message from the leader, ideally in person or on podcast or video conference, will prepare both employees and management for what lies ahead. Be utterly transparent about what you hope to achieve, but don't go into too much detail at this point. Simply inform everyone that their input may be solicited through surveys, interviews, or focus groups during an upcoming assessment of your current culture. Don't worry if some employees who are not selected for the assessment offer their opinions anyway. Accept them; strong, unsolicited opinions from anywhere are valuable. Not only does this whole assessment process give you valuable information, but it is the first step toward building acceptance and even excitement for the coming change.

Action Step 2: Nominate an assessment team

To enhance trust in the results, members of the assessment team should not be primarily executives or HR. They should be drawn from all levels of experience and the most important parts of your organization. The team will decide on the survey, interview, and focus group questions, as well as procedures for processing, analyzing, reporting, and acting on the results of the assessments. You might want to have operations lead this process if they are respected within your organization, with HR in charge of the execution. But if trust is an issue in your organization—do you think people have the courage to be honest or not?—then do yourself a favor and hire an outside research firm to help your team complete the assessment. The number of people on the team can be as small as five or as large as thirty; the number varies by the size of the company. Include people from all levels of the organization, from front line to executive suite. People of influence throughout the organization, representative of all areas, should be considered for the team.

Action Step 3: Gather existing survey data

Recent employee and customer satisfaction surveys can tell you a lot about the values gap. Exit interviews are also a potentially eye-opening source of information. Search for recurring themes: the top five scores, the bottom five scores, to start with. Are certain kinds of failures (or successes) mentioned repeatedly? Is there any difference between the responses of current employees and those who leave? A comparison between senior executive responses and those of lower level employees can also be revealing. Often the view from the executive suite does not bear any relation to what employees are experiencing on the ground. Use existing responses to create more targeted survey, interview, and focus group questions.

Action Step 4: Create an anonymous survey

You'll probably want to create a new anonymous survey, one specifically designed to determine the values your employees are currently living. Anonymous surveys encourage people to tell the bad news they might otherwise keep to themselves. You can take your current stated values and design questions to elicit how well they are applied in your organization by employees, their peers, managers, and executives. Ask general questions about how systems in place now—such as hiring procedures, work rules, and rewards—help or hinder the implementation of stated values in the workplace. And ask directly about values, too. For instance:

> Can you name our organization's values from memory?
> Are you rewarded for displaying the organization's values?
> How would you respond to [a specific difficult customer situation]?

And more specific questions related to the way employees interact with the organization:

Do your ideas get serious consideration by supervisors? Why or why not?

Do you routinely see measures of quality of service provided by your department?

Do you understand how measures of quality correspond to your work?

Are you treated like an adult professional at work?

Do you feel comfortable questioning a supervisor?

Would you recommend the company to a family member?

For more sample survey questions, see the Leader's Toolbox.

Consulting firms can help you conduct assessments. In fact, you may already use a firm that has a good culture assessment tool: Russell Reynolds Associates offers a tool called Culture Analyst; Human Synergistics and Denison Consulting also have culture surveys.[6]

If you don't want to hire a research firm, visit sites like Monster.com or SurveyMonkey.com, which allow you to easily construct simple surveys that are perfectly adequate for this purpose. No survey on values should be longer than twenty-five questions anyway; shorter is preferable. Surveys should include simple questions, with a few open-ended opportunities to share thoughts. Again, anonymity is essential, and collection of demographic information should be minimal—you are looking for a broad cross section of attitudes here, not specific issues. Set a short deadline for people to return the surveys, and compile the answers as quickly as possible. The answers will inform your next step.

Note: Be cautious that values questions avoid strong association with any religious or cultural mind-set. To help you avoid giving offense, ask a representative of each major cultural and religious group in your workplace to vet the survey questions (as well as planned one-on-one and focus group questions) in advance.

Action Step 5: Evaluate current values and behaviors with interviews and focus groups

Interviews and focus groups often reveal problem areas you would never have been aware of otherwise. At Florida Hospitals in Orlando, Florida, "we were already a top-performing hospital financially and in terms of clinical outcomes," says Sheryl Dodds, chief clinical officer. "We even had our values in place and people believed in them. But we had low employee satisfaction scores and turnover was high, particularly among nurses. What we found out when we asked was the concerns that nurses had. There were some real issues in the communications between doctors and nurses. Many nurses felt that the hospital and the docs didn't value them. And doctors felt that nurses didn't know what they were doing." She also said that critical incidents weren't being reported as they should be because of distrust among the groups. "Upper management had no idea how deep and widespread the problems were," Dodds says, because on the surface, the workplace was calm and efficient.[7]

Conducting interviews and focus groups will give you the opportunity to peel back the onion and get to the whys. With even a preliminary bead on trends gathered from the online surveys, you can start delving into potential problem areas with targeted questions. The intent of these sessions is to mine a cross section of employee opinion and develop a snapshot view of attitudes and employee engagement issues. You may want to use focus groups (of no more than twenty) for rank-and-file employees to encourage active participation and an enjoyable experience. Be careful about including supervisors or senior executives if your surveys have shown any level of distrust for management. You want people to be comfortable sharing what they perceive as the truth.

One-on-one interviews may be best for upper-level employees who may be harder to schedule for group work. These also work well with the rank and file when departments are geographically dispersed, although you should try to set up at least one focus group at each major location because cultures may vary radically. You'll also have to do more interviews and focus groups if your employees do not, in general, have e-mail, as was the case at Doubletree, where they also spoke more than a dozen languages. And if you have to hire language experts, do it. Also, don't forget second and third shifts. Their opinions are just as important. Which method you select for each employee included in the process will be a judgment call.

Who should be asked to participate? At the very least, a representative or two from each functional area should be included, with a good cross section of job experience. Do not exclude those known to have negative opinions. Your most valuable information could come from them. We've also had situations where employees realize that they will be representing their work groups, so they take the initiative to talk to their coworkers in advance so they can pass on their views. Encourage this—people will feel empowered by having the additional channel of communication. You might even want to invite customers to participate. Florida Hospitals included a patient who didn't have the best experience at the hospital. Later, the CEO said, "Having this patient here made the lightbulb go off for me in terms of the importance of values." And the patient himself developed a sense of buy-in from being asked, as well: "I will come back to this hospital," he told us after the interviews.

Each participant should be informed of the purpose and confidentiality of the interview or focus group. Amy C. Edmondson, Novartis Professor of Leadership and Management at Harvard Business School, has studied the risks and rewards of articulating values and found that one of the most important factors is to "create a sense of psychological safety. Employees need to feel that it is safe to express negative views about leaders."[8] I recommend kicking off the focus groups and interviews this way: "Thank you for helping us better understand how 'the real world' looks in our day-to-day operations. You comments will not be identified by name or position. What we want is your unbiased and absolutely straightforward answers to the questions we'll ask." And be sure your executives don't try to sabotage the process. In one hospital focus group, the COO came waltzing in and sat in on the meeting.

He knew exactly what he was doing, I think. Those people weren't going to criticize senior management in front of him—although some courageous souls still did.

The questions your team will ask should be primarily open-ended (answered by more than a yes or no) and speak to actual values or behaviors, not ideals. Some suggestions:

- Can you name our company's values?
- What do customers really like about us?
- When can you remember someone violating your own values?
- How are new ideas from employees handled by supervisors?
- What is your understanding of the business performance of your department and the organization?
- Are measures of service quality shared with you? How do you and your department stack up?
- What is the single most important thing that could be done to help your department provide better service or improve financial performance?
- What would happen if you questioned a superior's decision?
- What is the most significant thing that could be done to improve customer experience with our company?
- Would you recommend our company to a family member or close friend?
- What are the characteristics of someone you would recommend for a job here?
- Also include questions about compensation, performance review, rewards, communication, onboarding, and other such factors. Are employees satisfied with those outcomes?

Use your survey data to modify these questions or create your own so that your discussions are as productive as possible. But don't worry that you're not asking the right questions. Once asked, people will tell you what's on their minds. Your team just needs to approach this without judgment and with an open mind.

How do you know when you are done? For the survey to be statistically valid, 10 percent of the workforce must be included, although we typically get good results if we include all of senior management, a majority of middle managers, and a good sampling of employees. In practice, if you are hearing the same things over and over, you have probably asked enough.

UNDERSTANDING YOUR "IS STATE"

Once you are finished with interviews and focus groups, you can begin analyzing your "is state"—the baseline that reflects your company's values and operations as they are today. Your facilitators (or survey consultants if you hired them) are the best people to tackle the task of data tallying, and they should do it in a systematic way that ensures that no information is ignored. But they'll likely be able to tell you exactly the main findings of the employee and customer assessments even before they begin compiling data. If your company is like most, they will have heard many of the same words of complaint and praise from people in widely separated geographical areas and demographics. So it will be informative for leadership to debrief them every day about what they are hearing.

Action Step 6: Look for key words and trends in the data. And do it every day.

During the interviewing and focus group process, make sure your people summarize their notes daily. (Focus group notes are typically from flip charts used during the sessions to record group accords.) Then assign one or two people to pick out compelling quotes, trends, and themes from the notes. Also look for "one off" issues that haven't yet arisen in the corporate consciousness but could be important down the road, such as small failures in customer satisfaction. Just one or two pairs of eyes on the data regularly will ensure that significant trends are noticed in what could become a mounting pile of data. These significant factors can then be compiled in the familiar SWOT analysis form (Strengths, Weaknesses, Opportunities, and Threats).

Action Step 7: Publish your findings

Demonstrate that the Values Blueprint process is going to be about transparency. Share both the good news and the bad news that you uncovered. Too often management waits to share bad news until they can come up with a plan of action. In this case, the plan of action will be implemented almost immediately, as a values team starts to work on a Values Blueprint that will help create a better culture. Celebrate that as you release the results of the assessment. And identify specific areas that hold the most promise for positive results for the company. Employees want to know where they can look for actions to be taken on the valuable information that they have just shared with you.

What you learn—and what you publish—forms a baseline for your culture. Comparing focus group and prior employee satisfaction surveys can be very enlightening. A mismatch warrants a lot of thought. Later you'll be able to return to the results and assess how much improvement has been made.

THE ROLE OF LEADERS IN CHANGING CULTURE

Think of the businesses you know that stand out as examples of consistently high-performing organizations. You'll probably run out of companies before you run out of fingers on both hands. What those few companies have in common are leaders who find strong values to be important. Study them and you will find that the leaders drive the values, the values drive behaviors, and the behaviors drive the culture. In other words, leaders cannot directly create culture. They can only create the environment in which a great (or lousy) culture will grow.

If top leadership dictates what the values are to be, culture change will fail, guaranteed. In that scenario, other leaders, managers, and employees won't speak up or they will only say what's expected. After the Values Workout sessions we'll talk about in the next chapter, we advise our clients to live with the values they've come up with for thirty to sixty days before making them public to the rest of the organization. Are the new values something the leadership team can incorporate into their daily lives? In one company, one of the values they came up with was "humility." At the end of the values workout we asked if they could all live with their values, especially humility, because it's easy to say, but hard to live. They all said they could. But within six months the CEO began screaming at employees, as he had done in the past. After coaching sessions, he finally said, "I don't care what you say; I'm going to do what I want." Almost immediately after that, A Players started to leave. We also pulled out, and he was soon ousted by the board.

It's important to assess the current state of your culture, because a good, solid assessment of where you are now in terms of values and behaviors will make the process of culture change infinitely easier. Building on a solid foundation of knowledge about your organization's existing culture makes adjustments to it—even major ones—much easier to explain and implement. Even start-up companies, acquisitions, and nonprofits will benefit from this a priori assessment of the attitudes of their leadership and those they wish to hire.

CHAPTER 3

CRAFT YOUR VALUES BLUEPRINT

The Foundation of Everything

There is a reason why efforts to change company culture fail. When culture change is imposed from the top—or from human resources—it is likely to be meaningless to the vast majority of your employees. Your effort to change your culture is doomed from the start unless you can agree on the fundamental values that you'll be striving to live by every day. Conversely, if you can achieve company-wide agreement on the values and behaviors you want to share, you'll build a strong foundation for culture change and performance that will be hard for competitors to shake. You'll also attract and retain employees for whom those agreed-upon values are the foundation of sometimes astonishing behavior, as demonstrated by a JetBlue pilot who gave up an opportunity for his fifteen minutes of fame when he lived by one of JetBlue's values, passion, and one of its associated behaviors, championing team spirit.

This pilot was on a routine flight from Burbank, California, to JFK when he realized that the landing gear in the nose of his plane was not retracting. He flew low over Long Beach, where tower controllers told him that the nosewheel was rotated ninety degrees to the left, perpendicular to the bottom of the plane. That could have easily resulted in a crash landing with lives lost. This pilot, though, was able to make a perfect belly landing at LAX and no one was injured. When the news got out, he was called by Larry King, Jay Leno, and David Letterman, who all wanted him to be on their shows. He said, "Well, if you want the whole team to come on the show"—that is, flight attendants and copilots– "then I'll come. But I'm not going to come on your show alone because I didn't do it alone." Maybe that seemed odd to the television producers. Who wouldn't want to be famous? To this day, that pilot has never given an interview about what everyone in the outside world considers his own personal, skillful, courageous act of heroism—and he considers a team triumph. In fact, to JetBlue employees, taking individual credit for something would have been the odd behavior. That's how engrained the company's values have become in the JetBlue culture.

I believe that the attitude displayed by this pilot is the not-very-surprising outcome of basing your culture on agreed-upon values. This is the reason you want everyone playing off the same simple Values Blueprint. At JetBlue, we created a one-page Values Blueprint that identified strong values to inspire performance and specified the behaviors that would make that performance possible. Your own Values Blueprint is a promise you are making to everyone in the company. Of course, you are probably already making promises. Many companies promulgate some version of: "We will focus on the areas that hold the most potential for positive results and prioritize actions that will quickly achieve higher performance." Sounds great doesn't it? But isn't it just the same yadda yadda yadda that managements all over the world promise in their annual reports every year? With a strong Values Blueprint, on the other hand, you can base your promise on observed behaviors you know will lead to positive performance for your company. You'll wrap your promise around a set of inspiring values, behaviors practiced by A Players, and measurable metrics so that you can be confident that everyone knows how to help you keep your promise. Figure 3.1 shows the JetBlue Values Blueprint.

For more sample values blueprints, see the Leader's Toolbox.

jetBlue VALUES

SAFETY

- Commits to "Safety First"
- Complies with all Regulatory Agencies
- Sets and Maintains Consistently High Standards
- Ensures the Security of Crewmembers and Customers
- Never Compromises Safety

CARING

- Maintains Respectful Relationships with Crewmembers and Customers
- Strives to be a Role Model at Work and in the Community
- Embraces a Healthy Balance Between Work and Family
- Takes Responsibility for Personal and Company Growth

INTEGRITY

- Demonstrates Honesty, Trust and Mutual Respect
- Gives the JetBlue Values a "Heartbeat"
- Will Never Compromise the Values for Short-Term Results
- Possesses and Demonstrates Broad Business Knowledge
- Commits to Self Improvement

FUN

- Exhibits a Sense of Humor and the Ability to Laugh at Self
- Adds Personality to the Customer Experience
- Demonstrates and Creates Enthusiasm for the Job
- Seeks to Convert a Negative Situation into a Positive Customer Experience
- Creates a Friendly Environment Where Taking Risks Is Okay

PASSION

- Strives to Meet the Diverse Needs of Crewmembers and Customers
- Champions Team Spirit
- Craves and Delivers Superior Performance
- Enjoys Overcoming Barriers to Good Service
- Looks for Innovative Solutions to Business Issues

Figure 3.1. JetBlue Values Blueprint

You can't impose values from above, just as you can't just order people to lop a certain percentage of costs out of their budgets—that is, you can't if you want to thrive. No studies bear out the workability of either of those easy strategies. Yet, based on our experience with culture change, your company can almost certainly thrive if you change your culture to one with more customer-oriented, positive values and behaviors. Now you just need a blueprint to get there.

Just as you would not build a house working off only an image in your head, you cannot build a lasting culture without a written Blueprint. The values and behaviors you agree on, and the Values Blueprint you will create at this stage, will serve as the decision document for every employee. Everyone should understand it well enough to get it into his or her bloodstream, so it must be a simple and understandable statement of values and behaviors that your company aspires to. Yet it also must be comprehensive enough to speak to a wide variety of situations. In other words, whenever a decision needs to be made, employees at all levels (even the C-suite) should be able to find the right answer there.

A powerful decision tool, of course, requires a lot of effort to create. There are no short cuts to values clarification, although the Values Blueprint process gives a clear road map of how to get there. And by clarifying the work to be done, values blueprinting can actually avoid the pitfalls pointed out by former GE chairman Jack Welch and his wife Suzy: "When you're developing your statement of values, there are long, contentious meetings when you'd rather go home, and email debates when you wish you could just go do real work. On days such as those, you might wish your values were vague and generic. They can't be."[1] Half right, Jack. Values cannot be vague or generic, true. But if you've assessed your current culture carefully, you can go into the values-setting process confident that you'll have a workable Values Blueprint in just two days. Surely your values are worth two days to get the ball rolling in the right direction.

We tell clients that their goal should be evolving from their current "is state" to a "wow state," but each wow state will be different. Very few companies tie their values directly to behaviors, but, as I've been saying, it's an exceptionally powerful thing to do. If "excellence," for example, is defined behaviorally as "we care and we stop to assist others to be successful," outcomes will be a great deal different from the outcomes if we define it as "billing the maximum number of hours." And if you find some problems in your culture—as almost all companies do—the Values Blueprint is how you fix it.

Anne Haines, president of ACCION New Mexico*Arizona*Colorado, an approximately $30 million nonprofit lender, decided to begin the process of culture change in the face of an increasing number of loan defaults in 2005. The reason for these defaults was that the company's culture was based on implicit values that rewarded quantity of loans rather than quality. By rewarding individual performance and growth of outstanding loans, ACCION had developed a "disconnect between the value of Excellence and its emphasis on growth . . . Staff's own examination of operations found there was an erosion of culture."[2] ACCION began the Values Blueprint process with a two-day staff retreat. "Some really solid values and behaviors came out of the retreat that have become our anchors," notes Haines. "The behavior we call 'leads with responsibility, joy and fun' has been key to getting through tough times. It can be a stressful atmosphere because of deadlines and the economy, but this behavior [statement] tells us that during times of pressure, we should stop a moment and help each other find joy in the important work we do." Just doing that, she says, allows her staff to focus more on making good loans.[3]

THE KEYS TO CULTURE CHANGE: THE VALUES TEAM AND VALUES WORKOUT

The short amount of time it takes to determine new values and behaviors for your culture often astonishes leaders. After assessing your current culture, you should be able to publish a Values Blueprint within a month. There should be no tedious meetings, no teeth gnashing, no back-and-forth indecision about the right way to go. That is only possible, though, if you put together a Values Team that is seen as credible by everyone in the organization. And that means including top players from all levels of the organization, especially the front line. That team can then spend less than two days hammering out the values and behaviors that will inspire everyone in the company, no matter how large that company is.

In October 2009, leaders at 7,500-employee Juniper Networks, one of the leading information technology and networking companies in the world, decided that they wanted the company to truly live its vision: the promise to "connect everything, empower everyone." Kevin Johnson, new CEO of the $3.5-billion Sunnyvale, California, company, which designs and sells high-performance internet protocol network products and services, wanted to be the preeminent thought leader in network design. He also saw opportunities to grow rapidly and wanted to have the ability to scale to $10 billion plus in a short time, says Steven Rice, executive vice president of human resources. But with employees in Asia and the Pacific and throughout the Americas, he knew it was going to be difficult to keep everyone moving in the same direction, enthusiastically, unless changes were made to the company's culture.

It was decided that twenty-two employees from around the world would make up the team to work on values at Juniper, including young engineers who were new but brilliant, long-time employees (who were old but brilliant), the founders, the senior executives, and the new CEO. A Values Workout session was scheduled at the company's Sunnyvale training facility. The CEO began the process by talking about why the session was critical to the company's new branding, how it would better define the company to customers, and how it would give them the edge over competitors. The CEO tried not to drive the discussion but just answered questions as I walked them through the Values Workout. We talked about current values and proposed new values and then they went home to think overnight about what employee behaviors would best exemplify those values. A draft Values Blueprint that emerged after a day and a half was enthusiastically welcomed by the company when it was announced. Not bad for less than two days' work.[4]

Action Step 1: Begin the conversation

While you are going through the process of assessing your company's current values (described in Chapter Two), or immediately afterward, I always suggest a meeting of senior management to discuss leadership's understanding of those existing values, whether stated or unstated. Look at your current mission statement and stated values—make sure they are concepts you could "create behaviors around." That is, think about how employees could execute a particular value. What does "integrity" mean in the day-to-day life of your company, for example? Or if you've never actually codified your values, think about what your culture might be saying to customers and employees. Are customer service queues long? Do you give refunds only under duress? Or do people say great things about your products online? You also want to make certain you do not mistake results for values. For example, "growth of market share" is sometimes seen as a value. However, growth could be an outcome of several possible values, including caring and fiscal responsibility. Remember, a true core value is a specific word or phrase you can use to guide behavior and operational decisions.

It is important at this stage for the senior team to agree on a baseline:

- Which values do you believe are currently in place?
- Do those values actually drive behaviors?
- Are the current values understood by employees?
- Are senior leaders actually living the current values *themselves* or only giving them lip service? (A vital step where absolute self-awareness is critical.)

Having senior management buy-in is the only way you can be certain that any new or revised values will be incorporated into your daily operations and that people will begin to live them. As Joel Peterson, JetBlue chairman, wisely noted, "You need to be careful to [agree on] values that are going to be lived, because the moment a senior executive doesn't live them, it starts to breed cynicism."[5] I've seen instances of values-setting driven by human resources without the participation of senior or line management, and it just doesn't work. HR can facilitate the process, but if leaders don't support the process, it will fall apart.

In the case of JetBlue, we began at the senior management level with a conversation centered around a theme of "Bringing Humanity Back to Air Travel." We discussed what we did and did not want to emulate, given our own past experiences as airline passengers and what great experiences for our customers and crew members would look like. We ended up with the essential values of Safety, Passion, Caring, Integrity, and Fun. But we still needed to decide what those meant in terms of behaviors, and we wanted to involve our small group of initial employees in the process. So we created the Values Workout process to ensure that our best employees would contribute to the creation of our values. I have discovered that this technique for generating real buy-in makes culture change easier no matter how large or small the company.

Action Step 2: Select a Values Workout team

After senior leaders develop their thoughts about values, they should start selecting a "Values Workout team." The key role of the team is to work on behalf of the employees (and representing all levels and types of employees) to develop and implement the Values Blueprint that the company will use to improve its culture. Specifically, the Values Workout team will

- Assess the validity of existing organizational values as identified by senior management and through the assessment process
- Understand the current values and their place in the organization
- Decide whether new values need to be created, existing values need to be reinvigorated, or some combination of new and existing values should be developed

- Determine universal employee behaviors that will be associated with the new values
- Publish a draft Values Blueprint, the touchstone document that everyone can look to for guidance as you implement values-based hiring, performance, and rewards

The Values Workout team should have no fewer than five and no more than thirty people, no matter how large your company is. More than thirty becomes a very difficult group to manage; fewer than thirty is better. Tell prospective team members that they are committing to an initial two-day Values Blueprint Workout plus regular advisory and implementation duties for a year or two thereafter. To be on a team for several years is a big commitment, so you must consider who will be the most motivated to take on the task. Go both deep and wide when making the appointments to this team. It is vital that A Players from every level are asked to participate, from senior management to the most entry-level person.

Include people from corporate communications and marketing in the Values Workout team. They can help you create language for the values that is appropriate for your organization and will also help you better communicate your values further down the road. It is also critical that a good selection of senior leaders, including the CEO and other top executives, be a part of the team. At one organization we failed to get the commitment of the CFO, who was absent for the Values Workout session. This proved to be a strategic error. He was never fully committed to the outcome of the Blueprint work sessions and the values rollout. His absence, and the resulting resistance to helping with the financial aspects of becoming a values-rich organization, severely impeded the rollout and implementation.

Other stakeholders should also be considered for inclusion on the Values Workout team. Loma Linda University Medical Center included hospital administrators, physicians, nurses, department managers, technicians, and support people. Significantly, they also included a couple of people who had been patients in order to get their perspective. JetBlue's initial Values Workout team included aircraft technicians, flight attendants, pilots, and staff from the finance department, flight operations, and marketing. Each player is given equal input—it is vital to ensure that top managers all understand that they will not be first among equals, and even the CEO shouldn't try to direct the outcomes. To do so is to fatally sabotage the possibility of success.

The most vital criterion: the people selected should be respected by their peers. Having a team composed of mostly A Players will do that, and they will also generate enthusiasm for the project. A well-selected Values Workout team ensures that the values you implement will be relevant for all employees. Ask managers to recommend line people who are already outstanding contributors and will voice their opinions strongly. I have found that almost everyone, particularly among line employees, is honored to be a part of the team.

Action Step 3: Perform the Values Workout

Over the course of an intense two-day workout, the Values Workout team will define the values (at most seven) that are vital to your organization and decide which behaviors will give the most meaning to those values. Make it a mandatory off-site meeting for all Workout team members, including senior management. Also be sure to bring in people from other facilities, even if they are not in the same part of the world, whether they are in another state or another country, their input is valuable. Juniper brought twenty-two people to Sunnyvale, California, for its Values Workout from as far away as India and spared no expense making them feel comfortable. The entire session should be an electronics-free, closed meeting. (Except for dire emergencies, no one is to be pulled out. Your other deadlines are not that dire.)

At the meeting, the first task for the values team is to build on the preliminary work of the senior leaders and the company-wide assessment.

Make sure that participants have read the assessment results and have access to surveys and interview notes if they want to dive in deeper prior to the Values Workout meeting. As discussion starters, try the following questions:

- Do employees live our company's stated values?
- Do those values represent what we are today?
- Are the meanings of the values clear?
- Do our leaders support the values?
- Do our current values drive decisions made in our organization?
- Has our organization assigned specific behaviors to the values?
- Are our values integrated into the hiring, review, and reward process?
- Are our people willing to fire an employee who does not live by the values?

From this initial discussion, which could become vociferous, the team should develop a long list of potential organizational values. Everything is valid at this stage. Then break the team members into groups to discuss and winnow down the list. Try to put people at every level in each group and advise senior leaders not to dominate the discussion. Reserve at least a couple of hours at the end of the day to bring the groups back together to get concurrence on five to seven core values. At this time, the group will also come up with a working definition for each value.

The next step is to determine behaviors that exemplify the new values; this is an overnight thinking exercise. Your facilitator should remind participants to think about their own personal values in terms of how they themselves behave. Good organizational values are typically very similar to good personal values. Personal values are those beliefs that you hold so strongly that they drive your behavior, dictate how you interact with and treat others, and, yes, result in guilt when you don't live up to your own standards. For example, "integrity" in your personal life might mean telling the truth at all times or being candid with people even in difficult situations. A corporate value of integrity, on the other hand, could mean:

- Demonstrating honesty, trust, and mutual respect
- Never compromising values for short-term results
- Holding yourself and others accountable to actions and outcomes
- Following through on commitments and keeping promises

Overnight, assign a single value to each team member and ask them to think about (individually or together over beers) what behaviors in their departments would express that value. The next day should be devoted to getting consensus on the behaviors and refining your identified values. Sturdy behaviors—those likely to be most useful to an organization—must be:

- Observable
- Start with an action word
- Assessable
- Trainable
- Hireable
- Rewardable

"Some meaningful things came out of the discussion for us," says Steven Rice of Juniper. "Juniper has always had a strong team spirit and a collective mind-set. As we defined our values, they were all started in 'we' language rather naturally." Juniper's resulting values and behaviors, now called the Juniper Way, also had a strong togetherness element. The company's *two* core values (you don't *have* to have seven or even five) were "achievement" and "encouraging." The macro-level behaviors that came out of the Values Workout were:

Achievement

- Take on challenging tasks
- Pursue a standard of excellence

- Work for the sense of accomplishment
- Take moderate risks
- Openly show enthusiasm
- Know the business

Encouraging

- Show concerns for the needs of others
- Resolve conflicts constructively
- Help others to grow and develop
- Give positive rewards to others
- Encourage others

As you can see, behaviors at this macro level are defined as *minimum* expectations for employees who are living the values. Such definitions clarify the behavioral expectations and hold all employees accountable for the same behavior, which, in turn, creates a culture based on these values and gives a common base from which to grow toward a "wow state" and consistent performance.

Action Step 4: Publish the first draft of your values

After the workout, you will have a list of values and associated behaviors. This is actually a first draft of your Values Blueprint, which should be communicated (as is) to the people in your organization for comment, along with a thank-you, by name, to Values Workout team members. Don't be afraid of being inundated with suggestions. If your values team has done a good job during the workout, the draft will express many of the values your people already care about. The associated behaviors will often engender a sense of relief in many of your staff—"Finally, I know what is expected of us and it makes sense." Your inclusion of credible front-level people on the Values Workout team will also enhance its chances of easy acceptance.

If you touch most of your people during this vetting process, you'll engage them in the process and get the buy-in you need for the implementation stage. Pretty soon word spreads throughout the company that something very different is afoot. Plus, you'll soon figure out whether you missed anything important, because if you did, people will tell you about it, repeatedly. In our experience, the more people who are involved in the vetting, which should take about a month, the easier your Values Blueprint rollout will be. Think about it: wouldn't you rather be asked for your opinion on proposed values and behaviors than have them imposed on you as a done deal?

Juniper showed the values draft to 330 people at all levels of the organization and all geographical areas, or about 5 percent of total employees. "We walked people through the business strategy, brand personality and the new Juniper Way, value by value, behavior by behavior," says Rice. "And they were *honored* to be a part of this process, they were very engaged and, for some, it was a very emotional experience." Rice then incorporated their suggestions. Only at that point did he let senior management, those not on the Values Workout team, have a crack. "We told them that we just wanted to be sure, from an attitude perspective, that everything was appropriate, but didn't want them to be seen to be controlling the process." In fact, Juniper made a rather big deal of the concept of involving people at all levels of the company.[6]

Action Step 5: Publish your Values Blueprint and take it on the road

Based on feedback during the vetting process, the Workout team should finalize and publish a professionally produced, concise statement of your company's new values and behaviors. One example of a well-drafted and developed Values Blueprint is from Heritage Home Healthcare & Hospice (see Figure 3.2). The values and behaviors are simple to understand and are reinforced by color photos of satisfied patients. It also contains a subliminal suggestion about the outcomes to expect if the values and behaviors are put into action.

OUR VALUES

QUALITY

A level of excellence exceeding the expectations of our patients, clients, employees and community.

- Deliver and support best care practices to our patients and clients.
- Maintain and/or initiate safe patient, client and employee environments.
- Utilize new information systems and best practices to exceed industry standards.
- Demonstrate current knowledge of job responsibilities and resources.
- Anticipate needs and consistently acts in the best interest of our employees, patients, clients and community.

TRUST

Create relationships based on courtesy, respect, honesty and integrity.

- Always do what you say you are going to do.
- Establish and communicate clear expectations.
- Safeguard employee, patient and client confidentiality.
- Demonstrate a commitment to transparency.
- Create an environment that supports open and honest communication.

OWNERSHIP

Personal commitment and pride in the success and growth of Heritage.

- Lead by example.
- Hold oneself and others accountable for behaviors, actions and results.
- Show pride through appearance, attitude and performance.
- Commit to self improvement personally and professionally.
- Own mistakes and learn from them.
- Takes responsibility, offer solutions and follow through.

ONE TEAM

Working together to achieve the best results for our employees, patients, clients and community.

- Recognize patient, client and family as part of our team.
- Ensure success of the team by sharing personal and professional expertise.
- Partner with outside resources to enhance quality care.
- Share the credit and accept responsibility.
- Embrace and value diversity.
- Promote open and transparent communication.
- Celebrate the contributions of others.

CARING

Dedicated to compassionate care in serving our patients, clients, community and each other.

- Show genuine interest and focus on what is important to others.
- Always keep others informed.
- Be proactive by owning and resolving issues.
- Be sensitive, supportive and respectful of others.
- Go the extra mile to help others be successful.
- Contribute positively to the communities we serve.

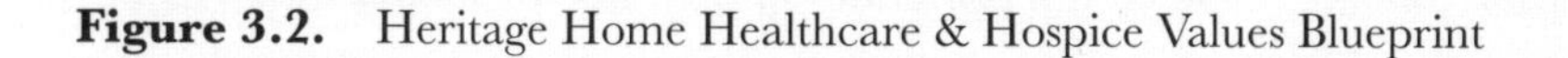

Figure 3.2. Heritage Home Healthcare & Hospice Values Blueprint

At Doubletree, the "Care Committee" Values Blueprint was published in the twelve languages employees spoke. More elaborate is the "Leading with Values" presentation designed by Loma Linda University Medical Center. Their Values Blueprint rollout included a glossy forty-page full-color brochure that defined—in very few words, mostly pictures—the values, behaviors, and changes in the operation that were being implemented, in straightforward language with a lot of white space. It was accompanied by a CD showing the values in action throughout the hospital. Employees received the CD at home, and it was accompanied by a bag of microwave popcorn. Loma Linda wanted to encourage families to watch it, too. Companies have also done this with just one simple sheet of paper and a few words.

The common thread between all of these presentations is that values and behaviors are stated in terms that employees at all levels of the company are able to easily comprehend and relate to. You want employees to understand that the company is taking the next step toward becoming a higher-performance and higher-spirited culture. As the Values Workout team begins the task of preparing the final Values Blueprint for publication, senior leadership should roll out another communications effort. The CEO should make a personal presentation to employees or create a video or podcast that trumpets the work of the Values Workout team and shows that leaders support the changes that will be required. If the initial effort will be confined to a few departments, leaders should present the timeline for full implementation and make sure the affected department heads also engage in a personal touch blitz.

Juniper pulled out all the stops. Thirty-one senior vice presidents, executive vice presidents, and the CEO all volunteered, many without prompting, to present the Juniper Way worldwide. Fanning out around the world in teams of three (which became known as the "Trio Tours"), the executives made seventy-two presentations to about one hundred employees at a time. Rice did eleven presentations in a week's time in India. "They just ate it up," says Rice. "They asked a lot of questions and looked for input on how they can help change how we do things."

Rice notes that the presentations were structured so that each one presented the values and behaviors in the same way, but each executive was given the freedom to convey their own personal understandings of the new approach. He tells of one who told about going to renew her marriage vows after twenty-five years. She said that her husband wanted to say the same vows again because he still meant them. But she said no—lots of things had changed in the intervening years and their vows had to change, too. We agree. The more personal you can make the presentation of the new values and behaviors, the more impactful—and less frightening—it will be to contemplate a wholesale shift in "the way things are done around here."

Juniper CEO Kevin Johnson also created "Unplug Sessions" to talk through the coming culture change. He traveled all over the world, setting up a stool and microphone in front of small groups of employees and simply saying, "Okay, what's on your mind?"

Without leadership support, employees will inevitably conclude that the Values Blueprint effort is a short-term program that will soon evaporate like others, producing no lasting benefits. Lower-level leaders need to know that they will be backed up by senior leadership as they challenge their people to change the status quo.

"Since we rolled it out," says Rice, "we're starting to see 'Aha!' moments. People now understand that we want them to be on the outside what they are on the inside. Who you are with your family and friends, should be what you bring to work. Now we want to touch as many employees as possible and are driving [our] behaviors into hiring, performance, management and leadership. It's how we do our jobs now."[7]

Action Step 6: Create a company-wide implementation plan and timeline

Your Values Workout team can now begin to focus on an action plan to ensure that the values you've set become a part of your organization's DNA. To make that happen, the values and associated behaviors have to permeate throughout the organization. At this point, you'll be getting started on the more detailed assessment of what micro-level behaviors and structures in your company are needed to integrate the values into your company's day-to-day work. Department heads and supervisors need to be intimately involved in this process. There can be no holdout departments whose leaders refuse to take part. If you do have people who stubbornly refuse to help execute these changes, you may need to move them on. In smaller organizations, the most practical approach is usually to begin the rollout simultaneously in all workgroups. In larger organizations, phased implementation is recommended. Choose two departments where the effort will have the most impact on performance and schedule a date in which implementation will start. We recommend two departments for the first phase-in so they can learn from and encourage each other.

Your implementation plan need not be complex, but it should indicate the order in which your departments are going to go through the process. A timeline, showing when each department will be coming up to speed on the Values Blueprint—including implementation of new metrics, scoreboards, hiring methods, rewards revisions, trainings, and other activities and celebrations—is also vital. Each scheduled department or division implementation should be phased sixty to ninety days after the previous phase-in so possible chaos caused by overlapping implementation is avoided.

You may have started the Values Workout process with a set of values that just needed tweaking or with the need for a major overhaul. Either way, you now have a Blueprint and a set of behaviors that can begin to inform every decision that is made at every level of your company. With a solid communication effort, everyone in the company should soon understand what it means to put the values to work every day. Leaders tell me all the time that they are amazed at how much difference it makes in performance to simply have people reading off the same page, especially when that page is the Values Blueprint.

CHAPTER 4

FILL YOUR COMPANY WITH A PLAYERS

A Values-Based Way to Hire

Once your Values Blueprint is in place, filling your company with A Players need not be an overwhelming task. A Players are the people who genuinely live your company's values, every day. They're not always the high-flying world-beaters, and they don't even have to be part of your leadership team. They could be the front-line employees who smile, who go out of their way to be helpful, who care that things are done right. They are employees who value what you value and want their company to succeed. They are the people who help great companies and great leaders reach their full potential.

Anne Haines of ACCION swears that hiring according to values was one of the most important changes her organization ever made. "We're now very clear about hiring people who align with our core values," she says. "We make our values very clear to candidates now—we've discovered that good fit is vital. People who work with us need to be good communicators who respond well to crucial conversations and are comfortable with change." ACCION is full of those people now.[1]

If I convince you of nothing else, I want to convince you to hire *only* A Players (as well as strong B's with the potential to be A's) *who display your values.* It is critically important and one of the most vital things that leaders can do in any organization. Too many businesses make the mistake of believing that hiring the best of the "available applicants" will ensure that the company is filled with good people. Or worse, they just hire the people they can get because they need warm bodies to keep the operation going. Judged independently, though, the applicants they are hiring would never meet the basic standards expected by the organization, and it starts to be filled by less desirable employees who were hired only to fill open positions.

The solution? Always hire A Players. You know what A Players look like. They are those people who are committed, dedicated, and successful in their jobs. They do more than is required, live the company's values, and truly add value to the organization. But they may not be "packaged" the way you expect. One of my favorite hires for JetBlue, for instance, is Lenny Spivey, a grandfatherly sixty-eight-year-old former New York firefighter who loves his job so much he recently told me he wants to work until he is eighty. One of my favorite "Lenny stories" happened just after we started flying in 2000. A woman on the flight, facing a family emergency, was terrified to fly. He arranged with the other flight attendants to be relieved of some of his duties and held her hand for most of the two-hour flight. He constantly gets complimentary letters from customers about his over-the-top service, and I'm sure that he has earned us thousands of loyal customers all by himself.

Your company would be far better served to wait to hire an A Player—or a strong B with potential to grow—than to immediately add a C Player. Put simply, C Players are people who don't fit in with your organization's values, so they'll never perform well for you. They might actually thrive in another environment, but they'll never shine in your organization.

Leaders must be willing to adopt a new hiring philosophy if they expect to lead high-performing, values-driven organizations. And that takes commitment to doing things right the first time. If you don't have a new facility staffed with A Players, you may have to delay the opening. You may have to pay overtime or be understaffed until you find the right people. You need to be willing to pass—always—on C Players.

You will also need to shift your recruiting strategies to attract better-quality employees and spend the time and resources necessary to get there.

Some authors, mainly academics, would have you believe that it is not possible to fill a company with A Players and people who have that potential. They would say that it is essential to pick "A positions" that you can fill with solid performers. These are the mission-critical slots that have the highest strategic impact on your organization and cause significant collateral expense when the wrong person is hired. In other words, they believe that you should concentrate on filling your revenue-generating positions with A Players and everything else will take care of itself.[2] In my own experience with high-performing organizations, they couldn't be more wrong. The most important positions in your organization are any that directly touch your customers. To your customers, your company is your front-line employees. If you want to attract and retain more customers, you must concentrate on putting A Players there first. But my contention is that your organization will only work as a well-oiled value-generating machine if you try, over time, to recruit, hire, train, and reward as many A Players as you can.

Filling your company with A Players usually brings substantial financial rewards. At Southwest Airlines in the 1980s, we were having a significant fallout during training. Many of the personnel we hired could not make it through training, and we couldn't figure out why. Then I was asked to create a behavioral hiring model around the attributes of A Players, interviewing people and selecting them *strictly* according to our stated values (the process I'll discuss later in this chapter). Suddenly the fallout rate dropped to single digits, saving the airline millions of dollars over time in training costs. One of the reasons Southwest now has the best record for safety in the industry, despite one of the highest takeoffs and landings figures of any airline in the world, is their stringent hiring model. Southwest also has the fewest employees per plane, which is a productivity measurement used in the industry. I would make the case that you can achieve results like these only if you have a preponderance of A Players.

But the most compelling reason to fill a company with A Players is to be sure that you can deliver on your service promise. I don't need to tell you that customers deserve top-level service; I believe that, and so do all of your customers. They will pick and choose those places where they feel employees are really concerned about their experience. Will you return to a Macaroni Grill because you got a free dessert after a twenty-minute wait? They did that for me, and I will return. And will you tell everyone you know about a bad experience? In speeches, I've told a thousand people at a time about an airline losing my bags, and I often name the airline. In other words, research has shown repeatedly that people will talk about only extremes in experience. If something really bad or really good happens, your customers will tell everyone they know, and that goes tenfold for the really bad experiences. So you want your extremes to be positive, and you'll get that from filling your company with A Players.

You may already be surrounded by A Players—or they may shine the more brightly because of their current rarity in your organization. Unfortunately, most companies acquire A Players almost at random. So having a lot of them is more a matter of luck than of planning or deliberate selection. More often, we reward our people for filling slots quickly with competent people. So why, even in times of high unemployment, when one might think it's a "buyer's market" in terms of hiring, do leaders still complain about the overall quality of their employees? It stems from a simple equation of supply and demand: A Players will always find the best jobs, and they'll keep moving around until they find a company that mirrors their values. Very few companies have a strong selection system that is built around the company's values to draw the A Players into their orbits and keep them there.

How do you recognize an A Player in an interview? Is it the man with the list of corporate accomplishments as long as your arm? Is it that articulate woman whose skills you desperately need? Maybe. At first glance, you might believe those people would be excellent additions to your staff, and your impulse will probably be to hire them right away, but I would say, "Not so fast." Remember, just because someone is skilled, talented, and experienced does not mean they are right for your organization.

A Players for your organization are people who bring *your company's values* to the organization and live them every day. In other words, once you determine the right values for your company, the key to successful hiring is to hire people who already believe in and display those values on a daily basis. In this chapter, you'll learn a powerful method for always selecting the right A Players for your company. Yes, you may have to pass up people you might have considered A players in the past. And you will definitely have to be more selective in your hiring. But in the end, you'll have a team of high-achievers who believe in what your company stands for and will champion those values every day.

VALUES HIRING IS A STRATEGIC BUSINESS RESPONSIBILITY

If you really want to fill your company with the best people, your Values Blueprint must be integrated into every stage of the hiring and retention process. Implementing an entirely new way of hiring is something that must be supported, encouraged, and reinforced from the top. In other words, everyone in leadership must understand that this step, perhaps more than any other, is a *strategic business responsibility*, not an HR function. This sense of responsibility needs to permeate everyone's consciousness and be constantly reinforced by leaders. Without this, the ease with which companies can slide back into the old methods of hiring is astonishing.

Dave Barger, the CEO of JetBlue, knows this well. Once, when he set about hiring a chief people officer, he met the candidate at home, in order to see how he behaved outside the corporate environment and whether he seemed to demonstrate the JetBlue Values of safety, caring, integrity, fun, and passion. "I decided it was important to meet him at his home. He was intrigued," remembers Barger. And the applicant was completely blown away by the next stage of the recruitment dance, he says. "Six Values Committee cochairs interviewed him, including flight attendants and reservations agents. Then he knew it was a very front-line-oriented company, and since joining us he has really embraced our way of hiring." Using A Players to hire A Players, in other words.

At Loma Linda University Medical Center, after the values hiring was put in place, the bonus calculation of corporate leaders and department heads was revised to make hiring and retaining A Players a significant factor in compensation. At the same time, turnover fell precipitously—from 18 percent per year to 1 percent in the ICU, for example—and the hospital's "patient engagement score" (a measure of customer satisfaction) rose to 99 percent.

One of our clients reported an "Aha!" moment when interviewing a person with twenty years' experience and a sterling resume. He said that previously he would have hired her on sight. But when he asked her to tell him about the specific steps she took to "increase revenue by 38 percent," she simply couldn't do it. Being able to articulate the behaviors associated with achievements is a key component of values hiring and one that traditional interviewing usually misses. "Wow, we weren't asking the right questions," the executive told us. And the light went on.

Even your ads on Monster.com and other recruitment sites will attract a better class of applicant if you make your values and the behaviors associated with them a part of your recruiting message. You'll simply attract more people "like you." You can also be alert for other organizations that share your values, even nonprofits and volunteer organizations, and encourage your people to recruit from those sources. And of course you should encourage your existing A Players to recommend people they know who are already living your company's values.

Satisfied employees are the best recruiters you can have, because they already know what it takes to do their own job. The last thing you want, though, is for C players to recruit for you, because they will recruit lovely people who are also C Players. And the last thing you want is to attract nice people who just don't fit in with your organization. Put a system in place now, including a reward system, to encourage even the lowest-level employees to give you names of great people to interview, maybe with a promise of recognition if they are hired. You should always be looking for great people, too, especially at companies who have the same values you do. When I was at JetBlue we often went after people at Southwest, kept after them, and tried to attract them to us. You should, too. And don't worry about being overwhelmed with applicants; you want to be inundated by the A Players. You should be so lucky.

Interviewing, though, is where this model really differs from common corporate practice, and we'll spend most of this chapter outlining how to implement it. The centerpiece is behavior-based interviewing, a technique that's been around for fifty years or more. What makes it work is that everyone, at every level, is hiring people based on the Values Blueprint. This tactic will allow you to identify people who have, over time, consistently demonstrated the behaviors you want to see in your organization. If caring is one of your values, you'll ask candidates to give an example of what they did when they had a difficult customer whose problem wasn't very urgent. You'll want to hear that the person took the time to solve the problem even if it was near closing time. Why? Because if they demonstrated caring once and can articulate it, they are likely, given a similar situation, to do it again. Past behavior predicts future behavior. At Southwest we even did a regression analysis of A Player behavior over a two-year period that proved that the most successful employees were the ones who could articulate past behaviors that matched with our values.[3]

But if you simply ask *why* a candidate wants to work for you, they're going to make up something. They will tell you all kinds of reasons, thinking that one of them is the one you want to hear. But if they can't tell you how they behaved in the past, they are not right for you. In that case, interviewers make a decision based on what they *think* the candidate would do or how they feel about the person. "A typical interview," writes Stephanie Clifford of *Inc.*, "unstructured, rambling, unfocused—tells the interviewer almost nothing about candidates, other than how they seem during a couple of meetings in a conference room."[4] But once the values hiring process is implemented, interviewers will all ask the same open-ended behavior- or values-based questions of every applicant and can objectively compare their answers. If done correctly, values hiring takes the guesswork out of interviewing. This allows the interviewer to make educated decisions based on a person's past behavior, rather than an emotional one. "[H]undreds of studies have confirmed that testing and structured interviews do a better job of finding good workers than regular interviews," concludes Clifford. "Given that, the gut-feel proponents start to seem like people who eschew antibiotics in favor of a good old-fashioned bloodletting."[5]

CREATING A NEW WAY TO HIRE ONLY A PLAYERS

Yes, I am recommending that you change the way you hire people throughout your company. And I guarantee that if you stick with this new hiring method for six months after launch, you will wonder why you ever did it any other way. After all, they've been doing it at Southwest for twenty years and have only 10 percent turnover a year. And when we implemented the model at Doubletree, turnover dropped from 60 percent to 20 percent, even among entry-level housekeeping positions.

"We started formal behavior-based interviewing when Ann [Rhoades] was chief people officer at Southwest," remembers Camille Keith, former vice president of special marketing for the company. "We discovered that interviewing was not so much about the answer as the attitude. Good teams are hard to build, but if you know what your goals are and who will behave the right way, you can get them done. We all have talents," she concludes. "It's a matter of identifying the talents."[6]

But I do not recommend that you convert to values-based interviewing all at once, company-wide. That would be chaos. Rather, you should create a values hiring team in one department, set up the values hiring process there, perfect it, and then communicate the success. Soon everyone will want to be part of it, especially when customers start noticing the difference in some employees. Here's how to get started, with a method that can be replicated (eventually) throughout your organization.

Action Step 1: Start with one key position in one department

Ideally, the position you choose should be vital to customers' perceptions of your company (represent high value to your company) and yet be hard to keep filled. Another factor in choosing the position is the cost of filling the position if a poor hiring decision is made. An airline might start with pilots. Some companies will start with the customer service agent position. At Loma Linda, they started with the "environmental care specialist," known elsewhere as the custodial staff. These, after all, are the people who were seen by everyone and trusted to create a neat, sterile environment. They talk to patients, come into contact with the public in the lobbies and halls, and must have high standards of cleanliness. But Loma Linda's turnover in their chosen position was more than a third annually, and employees were unhappy. A great place to start.

You can also start with a high-level position, as Southwest did with pilots. Whatever position contributes most to your turnover is critical to customer satisfaction, and would benefit most from hiring A Players is where you should start. To come up with the most promising position to start with, carefully analyze what position has the most impact on customer satisfaction, and therefore the bottom line, in conjunction with your operational and HR executives.

Action Step 2: Create a Values Hiring team to implement the change

Once you've targeted a key position to work on, a team of five to fifteen people should be chosen to work on the values hiring process for that position. Supervisors who oversee the job should be asked to nominate A Players to be members of this ad hoc team. People nominated should have a variety of tenures in your organization, to bring both a historical perspective and fresh ideas. You might even want to include a customer or two, as I suggested in the values workout process. Make sure that the individuals chosen are respected by their peers and interested in serving on the committee, since they will be asked to serve as peer interviewers down the road. My best advice is to take your time and choose wisely.

Action Step 3: Determine the key attributes of the position

Here's where top executives need to step back, although you should be aware of what's going on. The team needs to figure out what the key attributes of this position are. Some organizations refer to "attributes" as "competencies," but whatever you call them they cannot be determined from on high or even suggested to the team at this point, or the process will fail. Instead, the team should begin with a validation process—they'll interview employees they identify as A Players in this department. This will be about 10 percent of the relevant work force or all A Players if the department is small. They should interview several C Players, too, just to see what to avoid. Good questions to ask include:

- If you were looking to recruit a great person for this position, what would you be looking for?
- What makes you so good at your job?
- Some people have been unsuccessful in your job. What do you believe contributes to someone being unsuccessful in your position?
- A relevant behavior-based request like this one: Tell me about a difficult situation that you handled successfully.

The Key Attributes are different for every job and every organization. For some ideas about investigating yours, see the Leader's Toolbox.

From the interviews, which should last about forty minutes each, a list of common traits will emerge. The team should go through the transcripts or notes of these interviews looking for key characteristics of success, along with definitions. Typically ten to fifteen characteristics will emerge fairly clearly, which the relevant supervisors and managers should be asked to rank in order of importance and present to management for final vetting and narrowing to the most important five or six. Although this validation can be time-consuming, the involvement of those who actually do the job ensures that the credibility of the process will be high and that a sense of ownership will be established among the workforce. At Loma Linda, for example, employees in the department agreed when the key attributes of A Players among the environmental care specialists were discovered to be "customer focus," "accuracy and attention to detail," and "adaptability."

Action Step 4: Create an Interview Guide for values hiring

The Interview Guide makes a structured and fair process for values hiring easy to implement, not to mention almost fool-proof. It also makes it possible to concentrate on selecting A Players while minimizing the impact of "gut feelings" in hiring. Interview Guides have several sections:

- *Background questions:* to confirm that the applicant's technical skills meet at least minimum standards.
- *Complete stories:* behavioral questions aimed at eliciting stories about past behaviors or key attributes of the position. You'll learn from this whether the person can perform the job as an A Player. If a person can't get beyond generalities, the person is not a good fit for a values-based organization. And anyone who exemplifies the attributes will be able to give you numerous examples.
- *Organizational match:* behavioral questions designed to tell you whether the person exhibits the behaviors that drive your corporate values.
- *Saying goodbye:* instructions on how to close the interview while conveying the values of the organization.

- *Interviewer rating worksheet:* how well did the candidate fit the key attributes of this position? Because there will be three interviewers, ratings can be averaged and made more objective in this way. Great discrepancies in perception can then be debated and discussed.

The key to creating a successful Interview Guide is writing true behavioral questions. Typical interview questions are general background or "what if" questions. Behavior-based questions ask for *specific examples* of past behavior in relevant situations. Rather than "What are your greatest strengths?," interviewers might ask, "Describe how you handled a situation in which you experienced unexpected results." Behavior-based questions will always ask candidates to describe actions they took, either positive or negative. Applicants who cannot give complete stories in response to these questions are not the A Players you are looking for. Former firefighter Lenny Spivey, for instance, told story after story about his personal values in his JetBlue interview. One of them was about how his squad was called to a bombing in New York City, only to find there was not enough equipment to evacuate everyone quickly. But he heard screaming from four floors above, so he found a back way up and brought out two people who were calling for help. This story demonstrated that his values included the Caring that JetBlue was looking for, and it rather nicely predicted his on-the-job behavior. In just one small example, mentioned earlier in this chapter, he once rearranged his work duties, in flight, so he could hold a distraught passenger's hand during a flight when she needed it.

Using Interview Guides is vital to the success of values hiring and actually saves money in the interview process (after the initial setup and training period) because you can zero in on the right candidates more easily and minimize hiring mistakes based on gut feelings and first impressions. The Guides also ensure fairness and consistency—and avoid illegalities—by ensuring that all interviewers ask prescribed and agreed-upon questions, created by your best employees. It even creates confidence among candidates that they are being evaluated on their abilities and fielding solid information about whether they will like working for your organization.

> **Sample Interview Guides containing questions about each job's validated attributes ensure that the behavioral interviews identify the best candidates for each job. A sample interview guide can be found in the Leader's Toolbox.**

Action Step 5: Set up peer/manager/HR interview teams

Yes, I said peer interviewing: candidate interviews conducted by A Players who actually do the job. This is sometimes a sticking point for leaders, but a lot of great brands do it. Who can argue with the success of Southwest Airlines, JetBlue, Juniper Networks, Doubletree, and Loma Linda, all of which swear by peer interviewing? These are not any old peers, of course. These are your top A Players for each position. Some of them will be drawn from the ad hoc team that put together the key attributes and interview guides. Others will be recommended by managers of the area. In fact, peer interviewing is likely to become a powerful perk or reward as it is implemented throughout your company.

Slightly different Interview Guides should be used by the peer, manager, and HR, but all will contain the same behavioral questions about the three most important attributes. The rest of the attributes should be spread out in questions among the three.

> **A simple Interview Guide Matrix can help you plan which attributes of the job each of the three interviewers will handle. A sample can be found in the Leader's Toolbox.**

Peer hiring is the heart of this method and something leadership must get behind in a vocal way or it will fail. In one company I worked with, they continually came up with creative ways to avoid peer hiring. They even decided that panels of peers would be a good idea, but having three people do an interview at the same time comes across as unfair to candidates, who often feel like they are being ganged up on. Some employers use panels of as many as five peers; in our opinion, this loses the intimacy of one-on-one interviews that elicits better stories. Then they wonder why A Players aren't always the ones hired.

When I was at Doubletree we started peer hiring first among the housekeeping staff. Up until then, turnover had been astonishingly high. Then we began having housekeepers interview prospective housekeepers. And because they spoke multiple foreign languages, we allowed them to interview in their own languages. We watched in amazement. Not only did turnover decrease to single digits, but our housekeepers were coming in on weekends, not clocking in, and shadowing the people they had hired. They knew that their peers would hold them accountable for hiring strong players, but they also wanted to make sure that the countrymen and -women they hired were successful in their jobs.

At Southwest, we immediately proved the value of peer hiring by having pilots interview pilots. I found out very quickly that having HR call for background checks on pilots is very ineffective because of fear of retaliation in the small flying community. However, when we started having pilots call peers, we ended up gathering in-depth information that we would never be able to get otherwise. That included a mother who told us not to hire her son, a fellow pilot, because he was incompetent. When we started peer hiring at Southwest, we also compared the cost of hiring methods. Not only did turnover decrease, but we actually cut overall training costs, too.

For some ideas on how to structure this training, see the Sample Training Guide in the Leader's Toolbox.

Action Step 6: Train interviewers to evaluate candidates with their heads, not their guts

Too often in traditional interviewing, people get hired because the interviewer likes them or finds them attractive. Behavioral interviewing, based on key attributes, is intended to take that element out of the process.

But people who are experienced in hiring may have to be convinced that this method works better—and learn through practice another way of interviewing and evaluating candidates. Thus the leadership team should be the first group trained in this new kind of behavioral interviewing, in order to solicit their buy-in. Once word gets out that you are going to involve peers in the interviewing process, any resistance from line players will quickly fade. And, unlike much interviewing training, practice for values interviewing needs to be as realistic as possible, especially for peer interviewers. That means live interviews. In hospital settings, we have nursing students sit down in mock interviews with a team of three trainee interviewers: one interviews the students and the other two observe. Interns and temporary workers can be used in other settings, which also gives those workers practice for when they will want to apply for a full-time job with your company. Whoever you recruit to help your interviewers practice should have enough experience in your industry to give realistic answers. But they should not be coached in what to say. Letting things unfold naturally is a good learning opportunity for everyone.

Have skilled A Player interviewers from HR and operations do the training. The training should take place over two days, preferably off-site. Attendees will be given opportunities to practice the new interviewing techniques, as well as learn to apply consistent ratings to candidates and to be objective in their observations. In brief, the interviewers will give grades to employee skills, evaluate their stories for reflections of your company's values, and grade the candidates on the key attributes. The key to successful interviewing is learning to interpret clues and red flags; for instance, empty stories (in which the applicant relies on wiggle words like *usually, typically, always, would, could*, or *should*) or incomplete stories that seem to be hiding something.

You can help interviewers discuss their interviews and come to a reasoned consensus by providing them with (and training them to use) a simple Team Consensus Worksheet. A sample worksheet can be found in the Leader's Toolbox.

It is important to share with the trainees that it takes four to five interviews, using the Interview Guide, before all this will feel comfortable. Peers and managers have different problems, of course: for peers it is mostly a skill challenge—most have never been on the interviewer side of the desk before. The manager may struggle with giving up total control of the hiring decision. The training must revolve around the meaning of key attributes, active listening for value-based behaviors, techniques for getting people to tell their stories of past behavior, and how to evaluate what you've heard. Trainees also need to experience listening for likes and dislikes to determine how these line up with the company's values. For instance, if the company values team players and a candidate says what he liked best about his team is that "everyone left him alone," is he a good fit? Of course not. Believe it or not, this really happened to one of our clients; it was an excellent example to use in training to show that values really do stand out if you listen for them.

You can hire consulting companies—like my company, People Ink—to create and deliver values-based and peer interviewer training, but companies can also write their own custom training as long as they stick to the principles. It can help HR, if they are the lead on this, to begin actual values hiring in their own department before they begin giving the training. Just remember: The key outcome of the training should be an understanding that if a candidate is not a match with the key attributes and values *that candidate should not be hired.* Your trainers should get across the idea that it is much more costly and damaging to company performance to hire the wrong person than to do five or ten or twenty more interviews to find that A Player, whatever an A Player is for your company. If you or your team are resisting this—or peer interviewing—you should realize that it means you are not really buying into the idea that people are important in your culture. No matter what your blueprint says.

Herb Kelleher, CEO of Southwest, used to joke that this process was so stringent in hiring on behaviors that he never would have been hired at the company. He was wrong, of course, because the company was essentially built on the values he brought to the table. But to me it meant that he took the process seriously and was always monitoring himself for slippage into behaviors that were contrary to the Southwest Way, just as you should. He told me he could always see the difference between employees hired under the new model and the old way. He just didn't want to be one of "those guys."

Action Step 7: Communicate the change in your hiring process

Shout it from the rooftops and in the conference room that you are going to be doing your hiring in a completely different way. Your entire organization needs to be let in on the "secret" that you are looking to fill the place with A Players. You began by communicating the values process; now you must continue by letting employees know how the hiring process is changing and why. The entire executive team should endorse the process, and managers and team leaders should discuss its progress during meetings. Peer interviewing should of course be emphasized. Formal communications, too, should reflect the new focus: newsletters, your Facebook page, Tweets, FAQs, and even job descriptions should reflect how important it now is to match employee values and behaviors to those of your company. You also need to insist on employee feedback being solicited and pay attention to its content. Only in that way will the values hiring process continually improve.

THE BENEFITS OF OWNING THE NEW HIRING MISSION

Almost every company leadership team thinks that they are conducting behavioral interviewing. Management may insist that interviewers ask long lists of questions aimed at getting at skills and behavior when five or six targeted questions will actually do a better job. The technique has been around for a long time, but as you can see in the action steps, what I recommend goes a lot deeper than remembering to ask people to describe their past behavior. Still, some managers who liked interviewing the old way will always give you pushback about changing to a new system or will just fall back into habitual ways of doing interviewing if you let them. Remember the old adage: "If you always do what you've always done, you'll always get what you've always gotten."

My advice is to break the mold completely. Give your people questions to ask that will make candidates stop in their tracks. At Doubletree, where our values included flexibility, my make-or-break request was this: "Tell me about the last time you broke the rules for a customer or fellow employee." Watch out for the long silence or noncommittal response. The candidate who won't be a good fit for a flexible organization is trying to figure out an acceptable response that won't include admitting to doing any such thing. Encourage your people, when they are exploring attributes and constructing questions about them, to include at least one "conversation starter."

Vanderbilt University Medical Center actually compared methods of interviewing in 2005 to see whether they were able to select a better quality of anesthesiology resident using behavioral interviewing. According to the study's author, L. Jane Easdown, M.D., faculty members thought structured interviews "would be perceived as awkward and would eliminate the conversational flow of the resume-driven interview." They thought candidates might not like them, either. To their surprise, reported Easdown, "[M]any felt that additional positive information was elicited from most candidates, which gave rise to spirited discussion. It was reassuring that the candidate would excel in those areas as they had handled similar situations with convincing actions and outcomes," she said. In addition, she discovered that the candidates did not react negatively to the interview style and were, in fact, pleased to know "[what] qualities were important to our program."[7]

You may also be thinking that this process is going to cost a lot of money and take a lot of time. That may be true, but only in the very beginning. You *will* have to interview more people in order to find the A Players. Southwest now reviews some thirty resumes for every employee hired, at all levels. Oddly enough, the same number holds true for Doubletree and JetBlue. Improved ROI comes in lower turnover, a decrease in customer complaints, and higher productivity—simple as that.

The advantage of values hiring is that everyone on the interview team learns to analyze what they are hearing from candidates objectively. Interviewers learn to dig deeper to get to the behaviors that actually have an impact on job performance. You have validated attributes and set values to screen for. Your teams of three discuss candidates based on agreed criteria, rather than making a gut decision. The fact that you are asking the same questions of everyone causes this process to be perceived as fair and consistent, too, while making it hard to ask illegal questions. Confirmation of the validity of the process will come when feedback starts to arrive that the process is working. Peers almost immediately begin to perceive that the time spent away from their duties is worthwhile, as the people they hired come onboard. Line managers see the new employees outperforming those hired under the prior process and feel more comfortable letting go of control of the interview process. And the new employees themselves feel comfortable in their work right away, because their attitudes and behaviors were carefully selected during the interviews to match the company's values. Eventually you'll even spend a whole lot less time interviewing. Your whole company will be full of A Players who don't want to leave.

If you do nothing else, do this. Behavioral-based interviewing based on values is the most powerful tool you have to fill your organization with high-performing people. What makes it even stronger is that interviews are no longer based on vague questions about an applicant's greatest strength but are about behaviors and values that have been validated as necessary to the job. And when applicants are asked for stories that illustrate those behaviors and values, it actually becomes much easier to identify candidates who will truly strengthen your organization, not just fill a position. Add peer interviewing to the mix and not only do you have the most qualified people doing the asking, but you also are reinforcing how important front-line people are to the success of your company. That is motivation for positive behavior all by itself.

CHAPTER 5

LET YOUR EMPLOYEES IMPRESS YOU

Implement a Value-Centered Metrics System

Here's a surprising notion: the vast majority of your employees want to work in a place where people care about customers and each other, are fully engaged, take pride in their work, and feel the obligation to continually improve. In other words, they would prefer that you create what we call a *high-spirit culture.* They will even help you create it, if you let them know how. But you can't just take out a flip chart and show them steps one, two, and three—or worse, blast an e-mail to everyone. It is only when their rewards are clearly tied to departmental and organizational performance that they are more likely to think and act like owners. Values-centered metrics will allow you to direct their efforts by measuring and recognizing excellent employee behaviors, not just results. When you start measuring and rewarding the behaviors you want, based on your values, those behaviors will begin to arise out of the organization seemingly without direction.

A key component of the Values Blueprint process is to design simple metrics that allow the company's success to be easily understood from the front line to the executive suite. The idea is to fully engage every employee so they will help find smarter ways to conduct the business of the company and then to recognize them for doing so. Once that happens, you may be astonished at the lengths to which employees will go to make meaningful contributions beyond your expectations. A few years ago, the management team at Doubletree Hotels launched a program designed to involve employees in cost savings. In the catering area, they explained the exact cost of each item—silverware, plates, and so on—and emphasized how the financial impact could add up if they ended up in the trash because banquet halls were being cleared too fast. The message got across. The very next day when the manager arrived for work, he found a table that a group of catering employees set with eight full place settings, on display in front of the time clock where the hourly employees clocked in, so every employee would see it. The note on the table read, "We found this in the trash. Price = $1,200." If you give employees an understanding of numbers that are relevant to their jobs, they will eagerly get involved in helping you achieve the metrics.

We made a big deal in the company about the efforts of the kitchen staff. I learned early on that it was possible to inspire this kind of behavior in employees with absolute transparency, combined with simple explanations, about costs that they could control, as long as those efforts were celebrated or otherwise rewarded. When I was at Southwest in the late 1980s the cost of jet fuel got very high, and we continually apprised our pilots of the escalating cost. We also constantly shared that we needed their help cutting our costs without impacting safety (one of our values) in any way. The pilots, who were on a profit-sharing plan, responded by taking off more slowly, flying a little more slowly, and landing a little more slowly, which burned less fuel and saved the airline millions of dollars over the years without having an impact on scheduled times. By sharing this one metric, Southwest was able to convince most pilots to modify their behavior to make the company more successful.

What would cause kitchen workers to care enough to dig through the garbage for lost cutlery and pilots to take the time to save fuel? Instilling that kind of dedication involves integrating values into the heartbeat of an organization in two ways: first, by engaging employees in understanding how to keep the business healthy, and second, by incorporating values into the day-to-day operations throughout the organization. On the performance side, to help employees understand your business, more traditional metrics—such as occupancy percentage, ROI, customer satisfaction, and employee satisfaction measures—may have to be altered or augmented so that they speak to the specific values of your organization. You also must teach employees how to interpret performance metrics in terms of their own jobs. For example, baggage handlers who are aware of the load factor metrics each day will know how to manage their time to achieve on-time performance for the airline on a daily basis. This means you need to educate and simplify.

Despite examples such as this, executives and line managers are often skeptical that culture change has a direct impact on bottom line performance. As for what makes the most difference, Jody Hoffer Gittell, associate professor of management and MBA program director at Brandeis University's Heller School for Social Policy and Management, has conducted a number of scientific studies that correlate an increase in relationship skills with improved performance. As reported in her book, *The Southwest Airlines Way: Using the Power of Relationships to Achieve High Performance*, Gittell showed that in five critical areas (turnaround time, employee productivity, customer complaints, lost baggage, and flight delays), statistically significant improvements were observed when employees engaged in more frequent, high-quality communication about shared goals.[1] The hard piece—and the one that makes a difference between high performance and mediocre—is making sure that employees actually share those goals rather than just giving them lip service. That's where observable metrics come in.

The most effective way to inspire that commitment is with reworked or new dashboard metrics. You'll actually need to have two sets of metrics: an Organization Dashboard and individual Team Dashboards that your people can easily understand and work toward. When values-based measurements permeate your organization, you have created a self-sustaining culture based on conscious values. So it is essential that everyone in the organization understand the scoreboard and the rules if they are going to play this particular game effectively.

One of the paramount premises of the Values Blueprint is that when people at every level of the organization understand how it is performing and are given the opportunity to affect that performance, they become more engaged in the endeavor. One of the key elements in creating that environment is the development of performance transparency, both internal and external. The Values Blueprint approach is based on extending that transparency to front-line employees. When employees understand the meaning of key metrics—and have an immediate stake in the outcomes—they will have a greater interest in influencing them. When given the chance to influence the improvement of those metrics, they are likely to contribute in ways that will impact the bottom line.

USE METRICS TO MAKE VALUES REAL

Leaders have access to a dizzying supply of metrics—finite measures of performance over time of all aspects of the operation. Financials, ratios, and statistics, presented in charts, graphs, spreadsheets, and formal reports, all help executives keep their fingers on the pulse of the company. But to your employees these numbers are incomprehensible. Even if you pass out spreadsheets or charts showing your results, in an attempt at transparency, most of your employees will avoid even looking at them for fear of being bored to death.

Dashboard metrics, on the other hand, give your employees a limited set of relevant numbers to comprehend. Most of us primarily watch the speedometer and maybe the gas gauge on our car dashboards; similarly, giving employees a few "local" numbers to watch can be both informative and stimulating. Everyone can understand that pushing the speedometer to 100 or the gas gauge to E has consequences. Those measurements are metrics that are within the complete control of the driver, just as ideal dashboard metrics are for teams.

Less really is more when it comes to dashboard metrics. The fewer the better—certainly no more than two or three. Whatever metrics you present should be sensitive to effort—you want to make sure that employees can see their work bouncing the metric up or down and understand it with just a quick glance. Metrics that cannot be moved easily may actually cause employees to lose motivation to meet the goal represented by the metric.

You want employees focusing on producing products or providing services to customers, after all, not worrying about numbers. Leaders must do all they can to focus the time and attention of the staff where these will best benefit the quality of services and products. A good, well-chosen metric will do that, almost without effort. To be useful to employees, a metric must meet four criteria. It must:

- Be directly related to the work being performed
- Be simple enough to understand with no more than three seconds of thought
- Include a performance goal for a time period
- Change regularly based on the efforts of employees

For example, in a hospital, a good metric for nurses might be "call button response times." For doctors, it could be "patient waiting time from schedule to actual procedure."

Another department not directly involved in patient care might take "department cost per patient processed" as its metric.

Says Rob Maurister, EVP and COO of JetBlue, "With metrics, we try to be simple, simple, simple. At one time, we monitored twenty metrics with crewmembers; now that is down to five and will soon be three, which reflect our stakeholder groups—customers, crewmembers, and shareholders. We make shareholder value relevant to crewmembers with both metrics and profit sharing. On its Organizational Dashboard, JetBlue's metrics include: (1) net promoter score for customers (customer satisfaction), (2) net promoter score for crewmembers (employee satisfaction), (3) operating margin, (4) cost per available seat mile [(CASM, in airline speak], and (5) free cash flow."[2] Maurister wants to turn the latter three into a single measure of its low-cost culture and growing financial success by the end of 2011. When I speak to corporate audiences, I always ask them to tell me about their experiences on the airline. Inevitably, they tell me about low fares, always landing on time, always getting their bags back and feeling safe—in other words, their customer experience directly reflects JetBlue's values, which will cause them to fly again, and which should also result in upping the measure of financial success. That consistent record makes me feel good; most organizations would find it incredibly difficult to perform consistently for nearly twenty-four million people per year.

It is possible because JetBlue literally holds all employees accountable for the metrics, which reflect the values of the organization.

Action Step 1: Create an Organization Dashboard

The Organization Dashboard looks a lot like typical performance management, except with a lot more blank space. A Values Blueprint approach understands that most people's eyes glaze over when they see a sheet of numbers. They don't know how to interpret them and are embarrassed to admit it, so they just check out. This is true even at the middle-management level, to a greater extent than most leaders are willing to admit. Instead of your people seeing incomprehensible numbers everywhere, your Organization Dashboard will present only those five or so metrics where changes in employee behavior are likely to have the most impact. Out of the hundreds of strategic drivers that you could choose, these are the numbers you want employees to watch most carefully. The most effective dashboards clearly show the minimum, target, and stretch goals for each metric the organization deems most important (see Figure 5.1 for a JetBlue example).

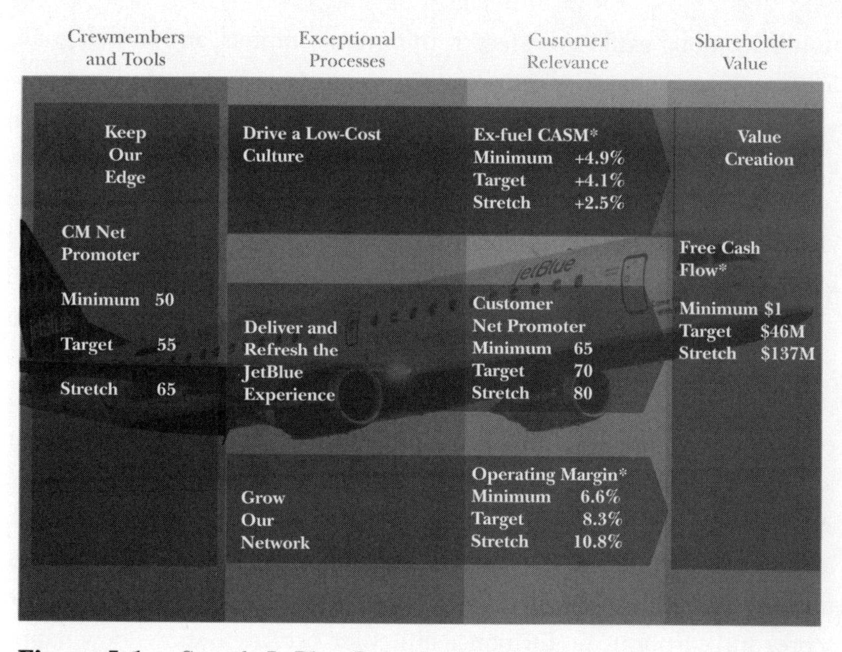

Figure 5.1. Sample JetBlue Organization Dashboard
*Based on operating margin.

Most of the goals will be in the areas of quality, safety, efficiency, and financial performance, but they need to be the most significant, *tangible* metrics you can devise, not just profits or net income. In the airline industry, you might choose on-time performance, baggage handling efficiency, employee satisfaction, and results on post-flight customer surveys. In fact, those are some of the metrics measured for JetBlue's Organization Dashboard. At JetBlue, the metrics are also further categorized by people, performance, prosperity, and shareholder value, each of which has associated numerical measures. In a hospital, some sample metrics include call button response times, patient census relative to goals, and department cost per patient seen. You will know, based on your discussions with the executive team, which metrics are most relevant to your organization. Be sure that constant updates to these numbers, along with reminders of minimums, targets, and stretch goals, are always available to all employees.

You may already have dashboards (sometimes called *strategic maps*) at the organizational level. This is something that few companies do well, though, because they get too hung up on financials—for any culture shift to succeed, you must align your dashboard metrics to reflect the values. For example, at JetBlue we quantify the value of "caring" through answers on our customer surveys. Six random passengers on every flight are given a survey consisting of four simple questions, such as "Would you recommend JetBlue to a friend?" An average of these survey responses is converted to a Dashboard measure as "net promoter score," a customer loyalty metric developed in 2003 by Fred Reichheld of Bain & Company. Additionally, JetBlue conducts a net performer survey twice annually with all employees to create an employee net performer score. We believe our research will show that there is a direct correlation between these two scores and corporate performance at JetBlue because it shows how happy employees are to work here and customers to buy here. We consider these to be breakthrough metrics.

Our net promoter target at this writing at JetBlue is for 75 percent of customers to be willing to recommend us, and the stretch goal is 80 percent. We're not there yet, but we're striving. Realize, though, that the idea is not to try to quantify the values directly. Rather, where possible, make sure that your Organization Dashboard includes metrics for every measurable value.

To create a true values-based Organizational Dashboard requires a rethinking and vetting of the current strategic plan or strategy map. Take the time, at a dedicated C-level meeting, to compare your strategic plan or map with the values. You want to pare down your goals into three to five dashboard metrics that could motivate employees. Ideally, it should require no more than two meetings to accomplish this. Your strategic planning process has undoubtedly produced many more metrics and goals than that. Worse, many strategic planning processes have become very sophisticated, with sacred cows that are difficult to challenge.

Financial people will typically say, too, that all of the metrics are important. And so they are. Help everyone understand that this is a "translation" process that makes organizational metrics accessible to the workforce so that they can easily see progress and focus their efforts.

Spend time discussing what truly drives each strategic goal, and make sure that Organizational Dashboard metrics are all focused around things that employee behavior can affect. Assure the finance people that all current metrics will continue to be tracked. In fact, your current strategic planning process does not have to go away or even be radically changed. It simply has to become more accessible to everyone in the organization. Remember that a page of numbers (or, worse, more than one page) will make even the most stout-hearted front-line person's eyes glaze over. Your Organizational Dashboard should fit (easily) on a single PowerPoint slide. You don't need pages of detail, although you can certainly have that detail available if anyone asks. We call that a *clear line of sight.* Your people should be able to explain to their families: "This is how my job impacts the organization."

What's vital is that you don't make your Dashboard goals too hard or too easy to meet. If they are too hard, your people will give up even trying to meet them; too easy, and they'll try to game the system. It helps to get input from a group of A-level front-line employees on the feasibility and potential wow factor of the metrics you propose for the Organizational Dashboard and whether employees feel they can move it significantly. This is a natural task for your Values Committee to take on. You should also run your ideas for the Dashboard past each function head to be sure it makes sense and is achievable. It behooves you to carefully evaluate the metrics chosen and the goals attached at this stage, because you'll be incorporating them into values-reinforcing rewards systems later.

Action Step 2: Create team metrics and scorecards

When employees understand the business of your company, they will be more likely to make a meaningful contribution beyond expectations.

Every team needs time-sensitive metrics to work toward, and scorecards, too. Scorecards report daily, weekly, or monthly progress toward the achievement of dashboard goals. We recommend no more than three metrics so focus can be maintained.

Less is more when it comes to team metrics. They must be:

- Directly related to the work
- Simple enough to understand with no more than three seconds' thought
- Limited in scope to concrete measures
- Numbers that can be influenced by individual and team effort

For example, the scorecard in Table 5.1 tracks three metrics that would be important to an HR department in a hospital. Separation rate, vacancy rate, and nurse hires are all metrics that the department would have somewhat in its control. Success rates are color coded so that the team's monthly performance can be taken in at a glance—green for great performance, red for underperforming, yellow for average. A closer look at the numbers shows that they too are easy to understand with just a moment's thought.

Employees will try to make those metrics move to meet goals if they seem achievable and contribute directly to the success of the team. Thus team-level dashboard metrics cannot be selected by higher-level managers and imposed on those below. If employees are to accept the metrics, they must have a sense of involvement in choosing them. People are simply more likely to buy into goals and objectives they've had a hand in establishing. The Values Committee, including senior leaders, should recruit "team champions" in each of the discrete workgroups in your organization as you implement the Values Blueprint. These champions should be A Player front-line people or supervisors. The champion will be responsible for explaining metrics and scorecards to their team and finding up to six people who will volunteer (that's critical—you must not draft them) to create the metrics for their team. We recommend

Table 5.1. Monthly Team Scorecard, Hospital HR

METRIC		All Employees	RN Only
Separation Rate Separations (Rolling 12 Months)/Average Headcount (Rolling 12 Months)	**Safe Practice** Safe Practice 5 and 6	18.36% - Actual 18.00% - Goal	16.04% - Actual 15.00% - Goal

METRIC		All Employees	RN Only
Vacancy Rate Open Positions/ (Headcount + Open Positions)	**Safe Practice** Safe Practice 5 and 6	6.20% - Actual 5.50% - Goal	11.90% - Actual 7.00% - Goal

METRIC		Actual RN Hires	RN Hire Goal
RN Hires # RN Actual Hires vs. # RN Hire Goal	**Safe Practice** Safe Practice 5 and 6	62 - MTD 356 - YTD	48 - MTD 266 - YTD

that the team include at least one front-line employee, the department manager, a supervisor, and an administrative support person. Including more than one front-line employee is even better.

Each team champion should take a look at what employees in the team do each day that is measurable. Tell them not to limit themselves to ordinary numbers: could "how many times you volunteered to fill in when others call in sick" be something to think about in your organization? The team should brainstorm to determine which ideas most closely fit the criteria for a good metric. With a manageable list, the team can meet as a whole or in small groups to see which of them has the most potential motivational value. A consistent method for measuring the outputs, as well as responsibilities for gathering the data, must be determined as well, if the information is not already being gathered. The team may want to test several metrics and scorecards for a few weeks to see how well they work in practice, but the goal should be to select just two or three metrics for each team.

When a final metric is selected, a short written description of it should be produced and agreed to by each team, detailing:

- An explanation of why the metric was selected: how it will improve performance, quality of service or products, efficiency, and general satisfaction.
- Specifics on how individual and team performance should move the metric.
- The minimum, target, and stretch goals: where should the metric be after a measurable period of time?

The metric needs to be converted to a scorecard as well, a graphic representation that clearly shows motion from week to week. Teams can get very creative in figuring out how to track their metrics in comparison to their goals. Scorecards should be designed by front-line workers themselves to be motivational, inspiring, and (most important) understandable. And they must move regularly or they will become just another piece of wallpaper, ignored and ineffective. People have to see improvement quickly.

Action Step 3: Track errors honestly

Everyone makes mistakes; to ensure that they are corrected, they must be reported and tracked. In many organizations—especially those focused on safety, like airlines and hospitals—tracking systems may actually result in the cover-up of mistakes. The key is to set up error metrics so that teams are not in competition with each other. Rewards for error tracking should never be based on minimizing errors, strangely, but rather on honest reporting and solving of problems and tracking of correction efforts. Otherwise, teams will be incented to "scrub" the data to make it look better, which solves no problems. In this area, dashboards and reporting methods must be focused not on meeting goals in lowering reported errors but in maximizing solved problems.

For many years, Chrysler has had a Product Quality Initiative (PQI) program in which employees are rewarded for identifying problems and suggesting solutions. Resulting quality and safety improvements are tracked via scorecards posted in break areas for each work team. Once solutions are proposed, the methods are evaluated by a Quality Team for cost and feasibility. Simple solutions are immediately referred back to the team for implementation, generally by front-line people themselves. More complicated and/or costly solutions are ranked by cost-saving potential and importance and implemented as the budget allows. Once the quality idea is implemented, it is reflected in the dashboard metrics and management celebrates the win with team members.

If more sophisticated error tracking is needed, as in life-or-death situations, I recommend a model developed by my partner, Charles Denham, M.D., of the Texas Medical Institute of Technology. To ensure that an organization is focused on rectifying performance gaps and is transparent in its efforts, Denham uses a four-point procedure:

- *Awareness:* There must be an awareness of the performance gap based on outcome measures, structure measures, and customer-centered measures.
- *Accountability:* Organizations need to tie personal accountability to a change of behavior if that is contributing to the performance gap and to be transparent about who owns results and corrective action.
- *Ability:* Make sure that staff has the skills to be able to correct performance gaps. It is not enough to be aware of them and accountable for them.
- *Action:* Make sure specific line-of-sight actions are undertaken in unison by all who need to change their behavior.

Denham believes that many more corporate executives need to be aggressive about performance gap management and be courageous enough to tackle performance problems. It is not as difficult as it may at first seem, and the solutions are often simpler than the problems would lead one to believe. Adopting values-based metrics will take many organizations a long way, Denham says.[3]

Action Step 4: Use games to reinforce behaviors

People love games. Even better, competition gets the blood moving and the mind focused on the metric. Too often, companies don't give their people opportunities to compete and win. The company bowling league doesn't count. I'm not talking about competition between departments or teams, either. That is always counterproductive. Every team needs to develop games that can increase involvement and fun, as well as give them something to celebrate regularly. To move the team metric in the right direction, teams should make up their own games that will reward people for doing just that. Done right, games can be self-funding based on the increased revenue or decreased cost represented by the movement of the metric. For example, at Doubletree, a Wheel of Fortune game was set up in the cafeteria for team or individual achievement. When it came time for a reward because a specific goal was achieved, the group or individual responsible for achieving the goal would spin the wheel and claim the prize it landed on. It could be a stay at one of the hotels, gift certificates, a personal service from the boss, or any one of a number of clever rewards that the employees expressed interest in when the game was designed.

What should the prize be for winning? Rule one: never reward with money. Money has no "trophy value" and is not really memorable. Awarding money also will lead to discussions about whether the money is adequate or not. Soon the focus is on the money and not on the game. The idea is to provide a meaningful reward but not to create a bonus-like reward system for every game. In fact, the major reward for any game should be the celebration of achievement when participants win, preferably with the participation of senior management.

With the money generated by the results of the employees' behavior, simple low-cost or no-cost rewards can be given based on the desires of the team. Some examples that have worked for our clients include movie passes, gift certificates, early release from work, pizza or ice cream day, or tickets to sporting events. Another popular option (for obvious reasons) is "Boss for a Day." The winner gets to ask his or her boss or supervisor to wash the winner's car, provide a shoeshine, cook a meal, or do the winner's job for a day. Very motivational.

We have found that almost any game format works—let your people be creative! But there are certain principles that must be observed in order for games to remain centered around performance and values.

- Games should be limited to no more than ninety days' duration.
- Goals for success must be achievable in the time allowed.
- Games and their goals should be limited to a single, natural team.
- Games should be fun and very visible.
- Rewards for success should be nonmonetary.
- A celebration at the end of the game is mandatory.
- Scoreboards should make monitoring of game progress easy.
- Teams should play only one game at a time.
- Goals are not "amendable"—never move the goal posts midgame.

For instance, a number of companies in which we have worked have designed games to decrease workers' compensation claims. Employees who have no injuries on the job during the week, month, and quarter put their names into a hat and then a drawing awards them various prizes weekly like certificates for days off with pay, day spas, movies, or "mystery boxes" filled with goodies, with a major prize drawn at the end of the year. Sometimes that prize has been a car or motorcycle. Although it's not intended to keep people from filing when they have a legitimate injury, it prevents them from submitting claims when the injuries are only minor, potentially saving companies millions.

Action Step 5: Set up systems to give authority

The easiest way to demotivate an employee is to give responsibility without authority. Good customer-oriented metrics should give front-line people the authority to apologize and make restitution in the name of the company at the first possible indication of a problem. When you are setting up new metrics, I recommend that you also modify your customer-management systems to allow front-line people more decision authority in customer service situations.

This worked out quite well for the Promus Hotel chain (Doubletree, Homewood, Embassy Suites, Hampton, now part of Hilton), where we gave front-desk personnel the authority to comp any person who felt wronged by the hotel with a free stay. We decided that one of our values was exceeding customer expectations; that's why we instituted this policy. Prior to that, employees had to refer customers to higher levels of management, and many customers left frustrated, which didn't help employee morale, either. Notes in every room still encourage customers to contact the front desk with any problems, which they can expect to be remedied right away. That policy resulted in $7 million in free stays one year, including an $8,000 wedding reception whose cost we absorbed after we neglected to reserve a suite for the bride and groom, who had to stay elsewhere. Were we nuts? No, as it turned out. We tracked those customers and found that they brought us an additional $27 million in the year after they received their "apology."

ONBOARDING THE VALUES

From the first day of work, you should be molding employees to own the high-spirit culture. For most of our clients, that entails a total redo of onboarding to incorporate a huge dose of leadership presence. Yes, you need to be there in person for every onboarding, and you need to tell your own stories. If values are important to you, you will make the time. Dave Barger of JetBlue estimates he spends at least 40 percent of his time in direct employee contact each year, including every single onboarding session in Orlando.[4]

Stories about leaders and employees living the values need to replace what most companies do to new employees: ad nauseam presentations about corporate history and structure, accompanied by a stultifying few hours of signing up for benefits. This is the best time to capture the new, fresh minds of employees, of course, so make sure you give them concrete, relevant examples they can use to help drive their own behavior.

Far better for new hires to walk away from the first day or two of work excited about getting started and understanding the business. Start with the values, of course, but then cascade down through the metrics, explaining in conversational terms what the goals are and what they mean for the health of the organization. Onboarding should make clear how dependent these goals are on the performance of individuals and how employees can benefit from participating. A similar explanation of work group dashboards should cascade throughout all departmental and team onboardings, either before or simultaneous with skills development.

Finally, new employees should learn how the Organizational Dashboard goals will be incorporated into their team and individual goals, so they know exactly what good performance looks like. Employees should not be expected to be accountants, of course. Nevertheless, a basic understanding of simplified business and performance numbers can help them better understand what makes their organization healthy. Employees need to learn how profit affects both quality and quantity of products and services. Basic understanding of costs and margins is essential to helping employees identify and influence changes that will make a positive contribution.

Redfin.com incorporates information about values and metrics in its onboarding through stories and discussion about employees actually displaying the values, then has a discussion with the new hires at the end of onboarding to see how well they've grasped the values. "It's the end of the quarter and a home-buying client is about to close on a $3 million property and Redfin needs to meet its revenue goals," a question on its onboarding post-test begins. "The client calls to say he isn't sure whether the property is right for him, and wonders if it is still possible to rescind the deal. What do you do?" By the end of onboarding, employees are expected to know how to apply the value of customer commitment to a discussion of this metric.[5]

Onboarding works best, in our experience, when a peer mentor who has an excellent handle on living the values and dashboard metrics is assigned to each new employee after the initial orientation. Both the values and metrics should be clear to the new employee, thanks to onboarding, and they will clearly be able to see the dashboards and scorecards in their work area as well. But it always helps to have a mentor reinforce what's expected on the job. If you reward peer mentors for passing on the values and behaviors to new employees, it will cement performance expectations all through the organization. Peers will encourage peers and monitor their behavior. They will also monitor your behavior. This cascade, both up and down, is what differentiates values-rich onboarding from the typical process—and is an essential reinforcement for the culture you want to create.

BASE DECISIONS ON THE EVIDENCE, NOT YOUR GUT

Since early on in my career, I have been an officer in some of the higher-performing organizations in their competitive sets in the country. Maybe it's a coincidence, but the majority of the executives in those organizations have taken value-based metrics seriously and pushed them down through the company so that employees, especially those on the front line, could take responsibility for their own astonishing performance. Yes, maybe it is a coincidence, but how likely is that? Getting employees focused on metrics they can affect with their own efforts has an almost magical effect on corporate results. However, it requires executives to adopt a different attitude toward decision making.

In other words, stop relying on your gut feelings. Decisions that are not made using metrics will simply no longer be acceptable in a place when employees understand more about how the business works. "Because I want to" didn't even work with your mom when you were a kid and is even less likely to now that you have pushed metrics down to the front line. But that's okay—and healthy for your organization—because now your evidence-based decision making will be transparently defensible to everyone from the boardroom on down.

Stanford professors Jeffrey Pfeffer and Robert Sutton observe that managers "can practice their craft more effectively if they are routinely guided by the best logic and evidence." But they also point out a possible side effect: "Evidence-based practice changes power dynamics, replacing formal authority, reputation, and intuition with data. This means that senior leaders—often venerated for their wisdom and decisiveness—may lose some stature as their intuitions are replaced, at least at times, by judgments based on data available to virtually any educated person."[6]

Don't worry; that's a good thing. In fact, if you look at organizations with the most satisfied customers, you'll observe that the leaders seem cut from different cloth than those at more average companies. There is a confidence about them and a focus on only the most vital decisions. They realize that they can trust their A Players to do the right thing, so they can concentrate on the next level of innovation. Still, leaders have a vital role to play in leading culture change, propagating it through the organization, and making sure it sticks.

Carefully defined metrics can make the job of spreading the word infinitely easier. If an employee can look at a screen or a wall and see a posted number that can be affected by today's behavior, they're going to know how to behave without being told. Reinforce those behaviors with fun activities like games and rewards, and the metrics are even more likely to move in a positive direction. Peers will start helping peers meet your corporate goals because everyone likes a winner. Even the language will change: employees will start talking to each other about beating the metrics and will get really excited to win, say, a J.D. Power award. Even decision making gets better, as leaders learn to concentrate on what's really important for company performance and front-line people earn the trust and authority to make their own decisions for the good of the organization.

CHAPTER 6

REWARD CULTURE CHANGE

Values as a Competitive Advantage

Recruiting and hiring A Players is just the first step in creating a high-performing culture. You've also got to persuade them to stick around. Research is showing that people really do stay in organizations where they feel engaged. A 2005 Maritz Poll of 1,002 randomly selected working adults found that employees who were satisfied with their employee recognition programs are seven times more likely to stay with their companies than those who are not.[1] Good people don't walk across the street for a dollar more an hour; good people stay in organizations that support their lifestyle and value what they value.

You can create a competitive advantage for your company among A Players by differentiating and personalizing your rewards package. Too many executives still see compensation and rewards as a cost sink and believe that they can't afford to adjust anything in that area. They may even make cuts in rewards as a cost-saving technique. The problem is that employees may not assign any value to benefits that you are spending real money on. Perhaps employees who embody your values and deliver outstanding performance would be content with a salary that is competitive (maybe not way above the market) if they could, say, work at home? You'll never know what employees really want if flexible options are not a part of your rewards package. For instance, we found we were spending a lot of money giving health benefits to at-home reservation agents at JetBlue when most were adequately covered by their spouses. And we were surprised to find that younger employees were content with catastrophic health coverage only, because most want coverage only in case they get seriously ill. You may be spending money on benefits unnecessarily—money that could be more profitably devoted elsewhere.

So just as hiring needs to be matched to values, so must performance evaluation and total rewards. When values-based behaviors are incorporated into the performance review, the organization is saying that values are important enough to be the basis for compensation. Total rewards, including bonuses and recognition, must also be aligned to values, as must promotion decisions and firing decisions. An employee who is not recognized for behaving according to the values of the company is an employee who will eventually stop believing that the values have any meaning whatsoever. And if you are lucky, that person will self-eject. If you are not so lucky, she will stick around and spread her disappointment far and wide.

Do you have to recognize every single instance of values-based behavior? Of course not. But review systems that will allow you to regularly monitor how well each employee is carrying out the values you espouse need to be in place. On top of that, total rewards systems must be remodeled to make sure you are rewarding those behaviors you value—and only those behaviors. The process will involve an evaluation of your current total rewards practices, as well as modifying, to a greater or lesser degree, your methods of evaluating, compensating, and awarding benefits. Some leaders wonder whether it is worth the effort. I believe it is.

I find it amazing how much money some companies waste on rewards that don't reinforce the behaviors they value. The old-school concept was that "time in job" is valuable and should be rewarded. But think about that: is the cardiologist with twenty years of experience necessarily more valuable than the new guy? Maybe not. The more experienced worker might be more technically practiced but not as familiar with new technology. And on the values side, either the experienced or the new worker might embody your values to a greater degree. The younger hire could have a brash, curt bedside manner, while the older doctor always puts patient comfort first. Which one is better for your organization? Impossible to tell, a priori. But now that you have a values system in place you know which one is better for your organization, and you can reward that person based on those values. One thing is certain: values simply will not stick if everyone gets the same 3 percent raise or the same rewards.

PEER REVIEWS MAKE A DIFFERENCE

One thing you must do to incorporate values into your organization is change your performance review process. Now. A wholesale redo from top to bottom may not be necessary; the essential component, in our experience, is that peers be included in the process. Yes, peers once again. You may be getting the idea that involving employees in all aspects of corporate operations is what I consider to be a good idea. That is absolutely right. For a good performance review, a multi-rater review is the gold standard when it comes to values, because even if one reviewer rates the employee too high or too low, the facts will emerge when the total picture is taken into account. And, as many organizations that use multi-rater systems have discovered, many employee complaints about the fairness of the process disappear, too, if peer reviews are shown to have weight in the review process.

How do you incorporate the values? Your Values Team should go right back to the Values Blueprint and determine how those behaviors should be demonstrated in each job category. This job will be made infinitely easier as more interview guides are created and used for hiring. A strong connection between the Values Blueprint, hiring criteria, review, and rewards is essential. A simple rating tool can then be created, allowing peers to rate the values and behaviors they have (or have not) seen demonstrated, on a numerical 1- to 4-point scale. When JetBlue was launched, employees were given cards to rate their peers with. It needn't be more complicated than that.

> **Peer review evaluations do not have to be complicated or lengthy, but they must clearly reflect the values of your organization and allow employees to evaluate the extent to which employees are living those values. An example of a Values Performance Peer Review can be found in the Leader's Toolbox.**

Action Step 1: Insist on values-based multi-rater peer review

To implement peer review, each employee and supervisor should jointly pick three to five people who are their "customers" in the organization. These should be people whose work the employee could affect in some way, and/or people who can observe the employee's behavior on a regular basis. Excluded, of course, would be people the employee eats lunch or carpools with; this is important in order to minimize the effect of office cliques and the chance of outright manipulation. Supervisors and employees should review the recommended peers together and should discuss what the peers know about the employees' work and how regularly the peer can observe that work.

Peer reviews can be anonymous if trust still needs to be built into the organization, but this is not absolutely necessary. Supervisors will incorporate the general sense of the results from the peer reviews into the employee's performance review, also noting any particularly outstanding behavior, positive or negative. Developmental coaching becomes astonishingly easy with these ratings in hand, because everyone is evaluated on the same criteria by people who really understand their jobs. Vague exhortations to "do better next year" disappear as if by magic.

Your A and B Players will respond positively to evaluation of their behaviors if the expectations are clearly defined. A Players will be gratified that you are recognizing their over-the-top performance. B Players will strive to perform at a higher level, many times directly modeling the behavior of A Players and eventually becoming A Players. C Players may suddenly start looking for new jobs.

One caveat: organizations using rating curves and grade levels to do performance reviews should seriously reconsider. If competencies are based on levels, some positions can never earn an "exceeds expectations" in their review because they are at the top of their grade. When promotion is not a possibility, flexibility needs to be built into levels. A rating curve is not motivational either, because a bell curve produces a large "average" area. Many employees who fall into that range end up feeling devalued, although the intent is to prevent rating inflation. An alternative to these forced ranking control systems is a calibration process in which managers dialogue and compare their ratings. Employees who are top performers—even if there turns out to be scads of them—should always be acknowledged and celebrated.

Loma Linda University Medical Center already had multi-rater reviews when I arrived, but according to Dr. Gerald Winslow, vice president of mission and culture, "we need help articulating the values in relation to it. Now we ask the people who work with our employees to evaluate how they live the values and the performance review process offers them a lot of affirmation, clarification of goals, and career development assistance." In other words, peer review is an excellent tool for surfacing behavior—both behavior you want to encourage and behavior you emphatically do not.[2]

Action Step 2: Start peer review at the senior level

Values evaluation from a multi-rater perspective is just as powerful at the senior level, if not more so. Employees are more likely to buy into the process if they see that managers and senior leaders are very visibly evaluated by their peers and subordinates as well. Leaders should also consider getting feedback from customers and talking about that, too, including gaps in behavior. In fact, when you implement this evaluation process, you should start with the top-level folks and hold them increasingly accountable for living the values. Even if you don't spread multi-rater evaluations to the rank and file immediately, the motivational value of hearing about it taking place at the senior level will be strong.

JetBlue has evaluated people at all levels against the values since the very beginning. As a board member and chair of the compensation committee, I am responsible for conducting the CEO's review. David Barger, the CEO of JetBlue, encourages us to evaluate him against the values and behaviors and to solicit feedback from various levels of the organization.

BASE TOTAL REWARDS ON VALUES

There is no better way to communicate the significance of values in your organization than to tie them directly to total rewards (compensation, benefits, and recognition). For employees from the top of your company to the bottom, total rewards are a bright beam of light that illuminates your culture. Your success, though, depends on your commitment to rationalizing your review and reward systems. Think about your current performance review and compensation process:

- Do we review actual outcomes versus stated individual goals?
- Or do goals somehow become "flexible" in the course of a year, depending on who is doing the reviewing?
- Are wage increases clearly linked to performance?
- Or do most people receive exactly the same increase in the name of fairness?
- Does everyone benefit when the company does well?
- Or are variable rewards and bonuses reserved for the executive suite?
- And, most fundamentally, to what degree do we reward the right behaviors through compensation and rewards?

Highly visible changes here demonstrate in no uncertain terms that you are serious about changing your culture.

Action Step 3: Map total rewards against values

The most fundamental step in creating a values-based culture is to review your Values Blueprint and determine where the values and behaviors you see there fit into your existing total rewards program. Map the values and behaviors in your blueprint against your current rewards program. Determine where gaps may be and which values you need to reinforce with new rewards in order to gain a competitive advantage. For instance, if your Blueprint says that innovation is important to your business, do you have programs in place that encourage risk-taking? Or do you punish employees for taking risks and make them accountable for every mistake? By focusing on making your values an integral part of your total rewards strategy, you will ensure that your organization rewards employees for the right behaviors.

We recommend that you spend some time reflecting on this with the senior management team. Then take the critical next step and ask your best line employees how they view the compensation and rewards process. This is just reinforcing that the rewards program has value to employees. Many programs are built around what leaders think are the right rewards, but you need to get feedback on what your best people think is valuable.

For a simple worksheet to help evaluate how well your current rewards line up with your professed values, see the Leader's Toolbox.

Action Step 4: Listen to employee opinions

Start with a survey of A Players to find out what they like about the current compensation and benefits plan. In large organizations, strive to survey people from every department, location, job level, and shift. In smaller organizations, get opinions from everyone you can. Questions should include level of satisfaction with compensation and benefits, perceived fairness, usage of current benefits, and desire for benefits not currently offered, such as widespread bonuses (bonuses paid further down in the organization than just the executive level) or paid-time-off banks. You may also want to test some of the concepts we'll propose here, including variable compensation and nonmonetary rewards.

In the case of one of our clients, surveys with employees showed that more than 50 percent of employees disagreed that "compensation is fair for the job I do" and almost 70 percent disagreed that "bonus plans are effective and reward the right behaviors." Results were similar for managers, only more so. Another factor that leaped out at us was that almost everyone said that facilities were encouraged (and reinforced by rewards) to compete with each other and felt that this was a weakness of the organization.

To peel back the onion and better understand survey responses like these (and you'll likely get more than you expect), convene focus groups, as well. Multiple focus groups—including 10 to 15 percent of your employee population, at minimum, with a majority of participants A Players—will help you understand precisely why employees responded as they did. Bring in people from all departments and shifts for a ninety-minute discussion. (Because of differences in benefit plans, managers may need to have their own groups.) A good discussion will cover the following:

- Which benefits are most valued? Why?
- What should we change or improve? Why?
- Which benefits encourage employees to stay here? Or it is just salary that keeps them here?
- Is the cost paid by employees fair?
- What new benefits would you like to see in the next few years?

In these sessions, allow employees to be creative about the benefits they want, although you'll want your facilitators to be clear that just because everyone agrees on good benefits to offer doesn't mean they are feasible, because of costs. Still, you shouldn't reject any deeply desired benefit or reward scheme out of hand. Companies find that there is a benefit to opening dialog about employee benefits; many employees are silently steaming—and plotting to leave—because the rewards they currently receive do not feel like rewards to them, and benefit plans do not meet their needs. We often find these focus groups provide a great opportunity to help employees better understand their benefits and also serve as a way to identify education needs.

A report on current benefits and the results of the assessment should be made available to all employees. Other useful information about benefits and compensation gaps that could appear in the report can be drawn from exit interviews, turnover reporting, employee surveys, and questions that are raised frequently in town halls or other forums. You'll also want to include comparative salary and benefit data from your competitors. Transparency like this will do more than anything else to convince people that you are serious about making changes. Employees will talk about it at home, too, which further reinforces the effort.

A suggested format for surveying A Players on their opinions of the motivational impact of your total rewards strategy can be found in the Leader's Toolbox.

PAY, PROMOTE, AND TERMINATE BASED ON PERFORMANCE

There is nothing like a raise beyond the norm to grab the attention of an individual employee; a promotion makes it crystal clear to all employees within line of sight what management wants to reward in an employee. In a culture built on values, those raises and promotions must be given only to those employees who are performing well while upholding those values. Otherwise, your employees will understand that your values don't matter. Termination, too, must be values-based. Yes, obviously, you still fire people for not having the technical skills to do the job or for any kind of malfeasance. But you must also fire those players whose values and behaviors are contrary to or undermine the organization. Even if their performance on other measures is adequate or even stellar. The top-earning salesperson who has no qualms about lying will only undermine an organization that claims to value, say, integrity.

And I would take that a step further: It is my belief that variable pay is the key to successfully remaking your culture, and—surprise!—your bottom line will not suffer. Somehow, paying people for excellent performance has never been a problem for me, although I know it is for others. At its most basic, paying for excellence means rethinking merit increases. A Players expect to be rewarded for their above-average performance with above-average compensation. If you expect them to stick around, a stated pay-for-performance policy is an absolute necessity.

Managers must have the authority—and the willingness—to award significant annual increases to the A Players and less than average or zero raises to others, even those with significant seniority. Zero is the kind of number that gets attention, particularly from your A Players, who will finally feel like they are being treated fairly when they hear about it through the grapevine that operates in every company. Being fair, after all, doesn't always mean treating people equally. In the best organizations it means treating people according to what they contribute to corporate success. True merit compensation, by recognizing actual contributions, rationalizes pay schemes and actually minimizes compensation cost. "Seniority smothers performance a bit. Why compensate someone more because of how long they have been employed? That can [tend to] drive a company toward mediocrity overall," Dave Barger, CEO of JetBlue, told me.[3]

I also recommend that companies consider another radical change in familiar variable pay plans: apply them as broadly as humanly possible.

Front-line employees have seen executives fattening their pay with equity plans and other incentives, but they rarely get to participate in those programs to a significant extent themselves. However, in companies where those programs are broad-based, results can be astonishing. At JetBlue, we started asking new hires what benefits would really turn them on. Flight attendants said they wanted more pay rather than stock options; pilots and mechanics, however, wanted pay plus stock options. We were firm believers that one size didn't fit all, so we decided to give them what they wanted. One mechanic told me that he was able to buy a home in New York City for the first time because we gave him stock options for his performance. That was a very happy mechanic.

Many people get promoted on the technical skills only, but you need to promote on the values, too, because those who are promoted become the role models that others will emulate. It sends a message when you promote someone who doesn't live the values—a message that you don't really care about values. I recommend that everyone being considered for a promotion or a lateral move be put through the behavioral interviewing process, asked the same values questions as if they were a new hire. It's not just the amount of time spent in a job; it's what people did with their time in the job that should be the key to promotion.

We once observed a hospital administrator struggling for weeks over what to do about a highly skilled but abusive surgeon. This man yelled at staff and used invective around patients. His bedside manner was nonexistent. The hospital had already gone through the values workout process and had put values-based hiring and performance review in place, so the answer was obvious to us: show him the door. But the man was responsible for millions of dollars in annual revenue. Eventually the problem became so bad that they did not renew his privileges to practice at the hospital. Very shortly afterward, administrators found that the revenue had been replaced by more surgeries scheduled by other doctors, and the hospital began to see great nursing staff return to that area of the hospital. We believe this will greatly improve their quality and safety record. "Why didn't we do that sooner?" is what they said to us.

A study of thirteen thousand senior executives reported in the *Harvard Business Review* suggested that "the most common reason for the CEOs' failure was that they didn't remove low performers from among their direct reports"—and anyone not living your values is a low performer who must be terminated.[4] It's really that simple. If building a culture grounded in your values is important, you take them into account in every pay, promotion, and termination decision.

Action Step 5: Reinforce through recognition

Many of the leaders we have met truly underestimate the power of a simple handwritten thank-you note to an employee. Recognition programs can be as simple as a well-timed "good job" comment from a supervisor—all the way to a very formal recognition program that results in a significant financial award accompanied by public recognition. The Values team can be tasked with incorporating values-based recognition into its communication plan. There is no better way to encourage the right behaviors than to recognize and reinforce those who model those behaviors.

A competitive base pay program is required to even play in the game, but the real upside occurs when organizations design variable pay plans and recognition programs that engage employees, truly reward individual and team performance, and link rewards to the business. Variable pay gives employees skin in the game, a built-in reason to care about organizational outcomes.

Just as every culture is unique, variable pay plans and recognition programs will look radically different even among organizations in the same industry. As you design your plans, pay close attention to what you learned by listening to employees, as well as the financial realities of your firm. With the goal of motivating your best employees to utilize their skills at the highest levels and to demonstrate the values—and to recruit others just like them—create competitive advantage through your recognition programs that are tied to your values.

Your organization can implement a broad-based variable pay plan if you have the dashboards in place, and clearly explained, so your people can connect the dots between their performance, company results, and their pay. Involving employees at all levels in the design of the final plan also strengthens the connections and gives you built-in cheerleaders for any new performance plans. The executive team should work with a committee of experts (consultants and/or HR people) to propose a preliminary plan. An employee advisory committee, perhaps drawn from your values workout team, could get involved at that point.

Eventually, I believe, most organizations can move to a system in which compensation depends 50 percent on actual performance and 50 percent on demonstrated values. "We thought it would be difficult to do this," explained Dr. Winslow of Loma Linda, where the total rewards now reflect this rationale. "Looking back, it really was laughable that we were basing only 5 percent of compensation on the behavioral components. And we wondered why people didn't do more to live the values."

Some companies really struggle with this concept. Basing half of compensation on something other than objective performance seems outlandish at first. Should it really be so much? they ask. "Well, yes," I always answer, "unless values aren't really important to you after all." This is absolutely the fastest way to drive change. In fact, organizations that resist this find that the culture change they said they wanted is extremely difficult to achieve. That is not a big surprise to me. By not tying values to compensation they are saying, loud and clear, that values are not important enough to drive your pay increase or bonus. Let's just put up a big flashing light to tell people: "You can ignore values. We don't care!"

Leaders can, however, take some time to make the full switch to values-based review compensation, as long as employees know what is coming. Many organizations take twelve to eighteen months to make the transition, establishing a hard deadline for the onset of the new criteria for review and training employees around the new way of doing things so no one is surprised at annual review time.

A CREATIVE APPROACH TO BENEFITS

Benefits are there to benefit your employees. When an employee really needs something that is not included in benefits, sometimes it's okay and important to be flexible. At Doubletree, for example, we had a rule that the health plan wouldn't cover in vitro fertilization. However, I decided to waive that rule when an employee came to me and made the case that the procedure was the only way she would be able to have children. There's a boy out there (eight years old as I write this) who thanks me every time he sees me. In another case, at Southwest, we had a pilot who crashed his glider into a mountain on a weekend and quickly used up his maximum health benefits on his massive injuries. In that case, we waived the maximum and paid his medical bills. And at JetBlue, an employee had a child with leukemia and needed to be in Boston for ninety days. So we gave him ninety days' paid vacation. In all these cases we were self-funded and able to do these things. There are options for doing this even if you are not self-funded, if you are creative and caring. However, many companies would never even consider this because "if I do it for Joe, I have to do it for Mary." Well, yes, if Mary's kid gets that sick, we'll give her the vacation time, too. This kind of flexibility around benefits builds huge loyalty and is well worth the cost. Companies who live their values commonly do this almost without thinking because it's just the right thing to do.

Undoubtedly, your organization already offers competitive benefits or you wouldn't be worried about peak performance—you would just be struggling to attract some good employees. However, I want to encourage you to think more creatively about benefits, because it makes such a difference in results. What I'm talking about goes far beyond fattening the medical benefit or giving more vacation. In fact, the benefits that employees value the most are sometimes *the least costly*, much less than traditional health and welfare: the opportunity to work at home, education completion benefits, sabbaticals, adoption assistance, pet insurance, and more. Many of these programs are simple to implement, have limited costs, and will be immediately popular, such as work-at-home opportunities and free tickets to events. Others, including such items as job sharing, may require enhanced communication and education to achieve their potential for motivation but may then be strong contributors.

> **For an idea-starting list of nontraditional benefits that have been appreciated by top employees at our client organizations, see the Nontraditional Benefits Chart in the Leader's Toolbox.**

If you already offer some nontraditional benefits, assess the utilization levels for these programs. Do some of the programs suffer from low utilization? If so, figure out whether it is because of lack of interest or lack of understanding or knowledge of the program. Then it's critical you take a look at whether your nontraditional benefits support your core values and thus have a reason for being. Meaningless, low-utilization benefits can be dropped immediately, without worry. Other nontraditional benefits, when tied to company values and communicated clearly, are likely to be wildly popular. You should be happy about this, since nontraditional benefits are often the least costly to the organization and usually just need a mind-set adjustment on the part of senior management in order to be successfully implemented.

Early on, JetBlue gave reservation agents the choice to work from home, and in so doing created an incredibly loyal and hardworking workgroup. Many executives find it difficult to believe that employees can deliver top-notch work without direct supervision. What did work-at-home add to costs and supervisory duties? Almost nothing. What did it add to mistakes and customer complaints? Less than nothing. Customer service ratings actually improved. It was a bit more challenging to let flight attendants share a job. We train both of the sharers and don't care who shows up to work. However, they do both have to make it through the behavior-based interview. We had one flight attendant who brought in three different candidates who didn't make it. So we carefully explained to her what to look for in a candidate. She brought in her son and they share a job now. And neither of them is interested in leaving us. We also have thirty teams of two police and fire employees who share one job. They make great flight attendants!

Another nontraditional benefit with a lot of upside is paid-time-off (PTO) banks. About one-third of organizations in the United States have already replaced traditional holidays, vacations, and sick time with PTO, particularly those that operate 24 hours a day, 365 days a year. PTO simplifies time-off benefits for everyone because all days off go into one bucket that the employee can use as needed. At places like Doubletree Hotels and JetBlue, supervisors no longer care whether the employee needs a mental health day or needs to care for a sick child. PTO gives employees added incentive to use their paid time off wisely and creates a sense of shared accountability. Employees can use their time off as they need to or "save" for long trips abroad by avoiding taking time off. Companies open for business on holidays may even save money by treating holidays simply as days that need to be paid out of PTO versus the traditional time-and-a-half premium typically paid.

Many organizations also use nontraditional benefits as an opportunity to give their employees an experience specific to their business. For example, airlines provide flight benefits to employees; hotels provide room, food, and beverage discounts at properties throughout their systems; consumer products firms provide discounts and sample products. Create a contest to allow your employees to suggest the nontraditional benefit they want most. Their responses will give you a clear idea of what might be missing from your current benefits offerings.

It is critically important that we think about benefits on an individual basis. Benefits can be motivational if designed fairly, but "fairly" emphatically does not mean equally. We want our A Players to know that we will consider anything they need if it helps them do their jobs better. Anything? Yes. I could have said, "Yes, within reason." But you can't automatically limit your responses when it comes to retaining your best people at all levels of the organization. How much value will you be missing, over time, if that person leaves for an opportunity that fits better? That's how flexible you have to be. Your people must have the authority to make decisions based on the concept of retaining the A Players, not because "that's not the way we do benefits."

As a matter of fact, flexible benefits often directly reflect the Values Blueprint. If anything is on the Blueprint that translates, directly or indirectly, into "we value our people," flexible benefits should be a no-brainer. Your Blueprint provides the information you need to develop a nontraditional approach to benefits. How can your benefits offerings be modified to reflect the behaviors you want to reinforce? You can probably drop some benefits, too, particularly those your listening tour told you are not particularly valued by employees. Basic benefits, on the other hand, may need to be beefed up to attract and hold A Players. Your efforts to implement nontraditional benefits programs will fall short of expectations if basic needs for benefits like affordable medical coverage and adequate days of leave time are not being met. Sometimes it is simply a lack of information or understanding that causes employees to undervalue benefits.

Action Step 6: Create total rewards statements to communicate the true value of benefits

If you don't already offer total rewards statements to employees, this is a good time to introduce them. And if you do have them, examine them for clarity and simplicity. Employees should be able to tell, with little effort, what they are being compensated for, what kind of variable pay they are getting and in what amounts, and what benefits they are receiving. Make the statements as plain-English as you can; if you have a high-language-barrier workforce, think about having them translated. Making it available online and in real time can be especially powerful. Otherwise, they should be sent at least annually to the employees' homes. Families can help employees analyze and appreciate the benefits they are receiving.

THE COST OF REWARDING BEHAVIOR

One of the biggest challenges of tying total rewards to the values and behaviors you want is making the business case. All organizations have limited resources, both staff and dollars, so initiatives undertaken must be values-based and have the most potential to improve business results. A change that may appear too expensive subjectively may actually deliver a great deal of benefit to the company in terms of soaring employee productivity. As you survey employees and make changes in total rewards, you should have a much better idea of what your employees will view as incentives to incorporate the values into their daily lives. Still, you need to evaluate the changes objectively, according to:

- Dollar resources: Budget constraints on total rewards programs, both long- and short-term.
- Resource needs: Do we have the staff resources and skill set internally to make the necessary changes, or do we need benefits consulting?
- Time constraints: Are there other initiatives and activities that are taking a significant amount of time right now?
- Benefits to company: What impact will changing compensation matrices, benefits programs, and other rewards and recognition have on outcomes—low, medium, or high?

The business case will be enhanced by a careful analysis of not only the obvious, direct costs and benefits, but also indirect cost savings from proposed total rewards changes. A consideration of opportunity costs, though difficult, will be revealing. For one thing, paying benefits to two employees who are operating on the C level is much more costly than paying them to one A Player, who is adding more to your bottom line anyway. You can afford to beef up your benefits somewhat across the board if you are going to be a lean, efficient company. Still, the real cost savings to be derived from tying benefits more closely to values and employee desires are in reduced turnover. Developing these cost-avoidance figures requires making assumptions around the number of terminations that did not occur because of improved pay and benefits programs. You might also want your finance people to take a stab at estimating the benefit to ROI of a benefits package that makes it easier to attract and retain key talent, especially for mission-critical roles.

Some organizations' finance teams maintain a strict cost-control process and will consider added costs and/or variation only during the annual budget-planning review. You know how your financial approval process operates and will have to structure changes in benefits to accommodate it. You should also consider implementing low-cost or no-cost adjustments immediately so that you can trumpet them to employees, while talking up improvements to come. You may be surprised how much impact they will have in reducing turnover among your best players while attracting more of the people you want to hire.

The competitive advantage of rewarding according to values lies right there: the people who can contribute the most to your organization are hungry to be recognized for their commitment to the values you espouse. A robust peer-review system allows them to be identified, and a total rewards package determined by values and employee desires reminds them of how important their contributions are. Under the ideal conditions for building a high-performing culture, pay, promotions, and recognition all ensure that employees put the good of the organization first. It just takes leaders willing to start putting the pieces in place. Even a little bit of effort in this area will increase employee loyalty that can manifest itself in quite unexpected ways. Try it and find out.

CHAPTER 7

ASTONISH YOUR EMPLOYEES

Inspire Culture Change from the C-Suite

Leaders are critical to the success of a culture change—just not in the way you may think. As should be apparent by now, leaders cannot build a high-performance culture through sheer force of will; neither can they just talk about their vision for change and expect it to happen; or even try to emulate companies that have successfully implemented a values culture like JetBlue, Southwest, Starbucks, and Nordstrom's, by borrowing a few good ideas and then expecting comprehensive culture change. No one should be surprised when companies fail to achieve an enviable culture when values do not permeate from top to bottom.

In contrast, a values-rich culture depends on leaders who mirror the values adopted by the organization and thus inspire over-the-top performance. The change starts in the executive suite and can almost end there. Live the values personally and you are halfway there, because employees watch every move in the C-suite. If caring is a value, then leaders must clearly care about their people. Really care—not just "demonstrate" caring. You can't expect someone to care about customers if they don't feel cared about. It just doesn't happen. When your people see you living the values and displaying the behaviors you all agreed to in the Values Blueprint, the lightbulbs will go on and stay on. Employees must see every member of the leadership team mirroring the behaviors in the Values Blueprint every time they have an interaction with anyone.

At Juniper Networks, one of their values is "bold aspirations," which their Values Blueprint links to the behaviors of "seek[ing] out big, bold challenges" and "embrac[ing] great ideas no matter where they come from." If the leaders at Juniper shrink from a challenge, perhaps in the face of ugly market conditions, for even a short time, they will undermine belief in those values throughout the company. At P.F. Chang's China Bistro, co-CEO Rick Federico lives the company's value of teamwork by rolling up his sleeves and helping with the chopping every time he visits a restaurant. Likewise, if one of your values is supposed to be fun, but work is serious drudgery for you personally, no one will live the value of fun at your workplace. Fun was one of our values at Southwest also, and our founding CEO Herb Kelleher was famous for having fun at work. That attitude of fun was so pervasive that we featured Herb dressed in an Elvis jumpsuit in our employee recruitment advertising. He was also known for showing up at baby showers for flight attendants in a bathrobe and curlers. And you should stop by the headquarters on Halloween if you want to see a CEO really cutting loose—the media loves it.

Even when things go wrong—especially when things go wrong—leaders must continue to behave as if their values depend on it, because they do. We practiced that idea at JetBlue from the very beginning. Shortly after we began flying, one of the wheels of an aircraft left the runway during landing. David Neeleman, the then-CEO, and Dave Barger, the present CEO, personally called all 162 passengers involved to apologize for the incident. (They split the list.) When Neeleman introduced himself on the phone and explained why he was calling, he received mixed reviews from the customers. Half of the customers did not believe it was him. A third of the customers raved when they heard it was him. Ten customers asked him for a job application. Bottom line: most of them are JetBlue frequent flyers today. This example illustrates three of JetBlue's values clearly: caring, safety, and passion, which both the CEO and president showed in this instance.

No, making the values come alive is not entirely your responsibility, and you can't do it by yourself. You simply create an environment for employees to thrive in. For example, David Neeleman and Dave Barger also created the JetBlue Crewmember Crisis Fund (JCCF) by contributing a large part of their salaries the first year. The fund is intended to help employees in times of need, such as those struggling with medical bills or parenting expenses or adoption. If they suddenly can't pay the rent or even reroof their home after a hurricane, they can apply. The fund is overseen by line workers who determine which employees merit the funds and in what amount. This was a stark example of the value of caring that pervaded the company.

Leaders are the strongest drivers of values and behaviors in their organizations. In a study by the American Management Association/Institute for Corporate Productivity of managers and directors at 1,967 companies worldwide, 61 percent of respondents said that actions by leaders were the most likely to influence the behavior of others in the organization. The researchers were not surprised at this finding, "given the hierarchical nature of most businesses today. Employees are obligated to take their direction from leaders and this includes not only listening to their words but, perhaps even more so, watching their behaviors."[1] Leverage that very persistent tendency of employees to follow the leader. Let them follow you to new or recommitted values and behaviors.

GIVE THE GIFT OF TIME

Your job needs to be focused on being visible and available to your employees. I often ask leaders to think about this question: "Could my employees pick me out of a lineup?" What percentage of your employees would know you or other members of the executive team if you showed up unannounced? If the percentage isn't very high, your employee satisfaction numbers—and your culture—are likely to reflect that. They are going to be able to recognize you only if you make yourself available and take the time to listen to them.

You may think you can get enough contact with employees by setting up video conferences and large meetings when you are in town. Not true. Employees want to touch you, they want to see you devoting time to them, and they want you to listen. Ralph Waldo Emerson once said that "what you do speaks so loudly that I cannot hear what you say." The principle is an excellent one to keep in mind as you decide how to spend your days. At JetBlue, Dave Barger devotes at least 50 percent of his workday to personal contact with employees around the country. Fifty percent! He has pioneered what he calls *pocket sessions*, informal town halls with every employee who is on the ground ("in the pocket" in airline-speak) as he travels around the country to the cities where JetBlue flies.

"I have a huge role to play in terms of communicating our values, and it starts with who we hire and fire," Barger told me recently. "But even more significant, when we talk about keeping talent and aligning them to the values, is to spend more than half your time tied into interactions with the human capital of the company. It's easy to 'fly the conference room,' but not useful. You are both teaching and learning when you talk about revenue and costs with a group of people in a break room. The ideas you get are so fresh—things you wouldn't learn unless you were listening." Barger mentioned that crew members in Buffalo recently suggested JetBlue should fly direct to Las Vegas because we were conceding that business to Southwest by not doing so, and they felt we could do it just as cheaply. "And they were right."[2]

Barger—like his predecessor at JetBlue, Dave Neeleman, and Herb Kelleher, former CEO of Southwest—is almost obsessive about getting one-on-one time with employees. He'll fly in the cockpit to get a chance to talk with the pilots, he'll sling bags for a day, and he'll service drinks, peanuts, and chips. He has also continued a tradition started by Neeleman of letting flight attendants from *other* airlines "jump seat" on JetBlue flights. In other words, when there was room in the flight attendants' jump seats (folding seats in the back reserved exclusively for the flight's crew), flight attendants from other airlines could fill them if they needed to get to work or home when their own airline couldn't accommodate them. It is perfectly legal, but the other airlines didn't like it because there was no formal agreement in place. Neeleman received a call from the chairman of United Airlines at the time, saying that he didn't appreciate the practice. David's response was: "You run your airline; I'll run mine." We continued to allow them to jump seat, and word got around quickly about how JetBlue treats its people. Probably not surprising, either, that we get thirty thousand applications a year, many from experienced flight attendants. Is there any service that you could extend to the employees of your rivals that would help you recruit their best players? You'll know if you listen.

Action Step 1: Set up leader rounds, pocket sessions, and other leadership listening systems

Find the influencers. The best CEOs I know do "rounds" on a continuous basis. At JetBlue, we have a monthly TLC ("the leadership connection") requirement. This means that all of our managers, directors, and officers have to set aside specific, uncancellable times to walk the floors, work the gates, and sling bags alongside front-line employees. And one of my heroes is Howard Schultz, who visits twenty-five Starbucks stores per week. He never veers from that, and he says he learns more from the field than he'll ever learn in the C-suite. But just as some doctors are better at rounds than others, it matters what you do while you're out there. You could be showing your face, but like a doctor who never has time to listen to the nurses or the patients, you can do more harm than good by "jogging" your way through this exercise. People need to know that you're listening. Yes, take notes. And, yes, get back to people with answers.

In these communication sessions, you should just sit with whoever drives the organization—pilots, nurses, customer service people, line workers, the person in accounting who corrects the mistakes on vendor invoices, truck drivers—and listen. A delivery guy on a truck learns a lot from customers; have you learned anything from him lately? This may sound time-consuming, but it really is only at first. Once you figure out who the *influencers* are, you can concentrate the bulk of your efforts on them. They are the employees who ask questions, have suggestions, and provide feedback with the best intentions. Some of them are leaders in the making, and they have the greatest influence over their fellow employees. Listen to them, and you'll be listening to almost everyone. Speak to the quiet ones, too. You'll never know who you will learn the most from until you do. "You will hear criticism," says JetBlue CEO Barger, "and it may hurt a bit, but it is being said out on the floor, so you might as well be part of the conversation."[3]

Richard Huseman, Ph.D., and colleagues at the Baptist Health Care Leadership Institute urge leaders to make rounding a planned event with goals and objectives. "Before rounding, leaders should ask themselves: How will I use these interactions to inform and engage my people? In what ways can I encourage and praise my team? And how can I use my rounds to help build trusting relationships between my employees and myself?"[4] Excellent questions.

On your version of rounds, you also have the opportunity to observe problems and engage employees to brainstorm solutions. You can also instantly reward excellent behavior with a kind word of praise. And you can pitch in to provide an extra body when service problems arise. Trust me, you'll be appreciated for your efforts. Leaders should also increase more formal and regular interaction with new employees. Several companies I have worked with have instituted new hire roundtables, where the CEOs sit down with new hires for a no-holds-barred discussion in the first ninety days of their employment. Other organizations, particularly hospitals, sponsor lunches with top leaders to get long-time employees fired up and engaged once again. These lunches are most effective if the leaders spend the first five or ten minutes demonstrating that they know what is going on in the department or division, commenting on how it is living up to the values and metrics, and then keeping quiet and taking notes.

MAKE GIVING FEEDBACK EASY

Just listening at town halls and informal rounds is not enough, though. There must be systems in place to allow great ideas to percolate up into your decision-making process. Leaders need information from front-line employees in order to make effective decisions. When leaders are out of touch with the realities of the operations, they often make decisions based on second-hand information that has been filtered through layers of management, removing its important nuances. The obvious message is, unless leaders have access to the people on the front lines—people who know better than anyone else how those jobs could be improved—many innovations will be lost.

Action Step 2: Create a simple process for giving feedback

The CEO and other top leaders should constantly promote the notion that they want to hear about better ways to do things. Astonish your employees by offering an online system for idea submissions aimed at convincing these idea-generators that they are vital to the success of the business. Your system should have these three simple components:

- *A simple cost-benefit analysis.* Employees should be required to explain why they believe that it will save costs or increase revenues—or both—if their idea is implemented. This approach filters out many of the "crank" ideas and encourages front-line employees to think in terms of return on investment and other important metrics.
- *Responsiveness.* We recommend that ideas be acknowledged by leaders within seven days. Estimate when a final response can be made. Share investigative results with the employees; get them involved in the investigation itself if possible.
- *Shared results.* Within the time promised, employees must be informed of the disposition of their idea during the review. Will it be

implemented? Why or why not? An excellent way to build trust and open lines of communication is to have senior leaders call the employee who submitted the idea and thank him or her personally, whether or not the idea is adopted. The personal touch helps make clear that leaders genuinely appreciate and encourage input from the front lines.

In your communications with employees, be sure to also include stories about successful ideas and how they worked their way through your system.

LIVE THE VALUES, TELL THE STORIES

Being a corporate leader is the hardest job anyone can do. You have to be humble and confident, a bold problem solver and an empathic listener. Plus you need to make sure that a huge enterprise stays on track, bests its competition, and delivers solid returns to its investors. Is it any wonder you sometimes have bad days? Unfortunately, leaders don't get to have a bad day when it comes to living the values. You simply don't get a pass to stop caring, or having fun, or striving for top-notch safety. Whatever your company's values are, if you want your employees to live them every day, then so must you.

As a matter of fact, leaders need to be seen as living the values 110 percent. Because of our value of caring, we had a rule at JetBlue that managers and executives had to respond within twenty-four hours to any employee concern that came across their desks. Note, we said "respond," not "solve." The response alone, however, was often enough to quiet the concern, and demonstrate caring, as long as the problem was eventually dealt with. Executives who catch themselves living the values also create a basket of stories they can pull out when necessary to reinforce the values. Joel Peterson, chairman of JetBlue, calls storytelling the most powerful communications tool that companies have to illustrate their culture. "You must tell your stories of success through values over and over again," he says. "These stories become part of the folklore of the company, a 'creation myth' for the culture, that explains to both insiders and outsiders why things are the way they are." You tell these stories in speeches and training, yet they are even more important in one-on-one interactions. "At the granular level," continues Peterson, "even in private conversation, you must always reinforce the values with stories of your personal stake in living them. If word gets around that you don't [live them], destruction of values begins."[5]

Action Step 3: Base your actions on the values; let your values shine through your actions

More than anyone else in the organization, then, the top leaders must discipline themselves to step back from any contemplated action and map its anticipated consequences against the values. How will this affect people in the organization and its customers? Are those effects in keeping with our Values Blueprint? Leaders who truly believe in the values will set ego aside, even if the idea contemplated is theirs and it's being shot down, and do what's best for the organization. In fact, as Peter Drucker famously said in his 1990 book *Managing the Non-Profit Organization:* "The leaders who work most effectively . . . never say 'I.' And that's not because they've trained themselves never to say 'I.' They don't think 'I.' They think 'we.' They think 'team.'"[6]

Even more so today, executives must continually model the behaviors they want to see in those who report to them. You don't have to wear your values on your sleeve, though; many leaders model great behavior in quite subtle ways.

Employees know you are living the values when you go the extra mile. Howard Schultz, CEO of Starbucks, was thousands of miles away when one of his managers was shot and killed at a store on the Pacific Coast. He immediately chartered a plane and flew there, spending a week filling in for the man, attending the funeral, and spending time with family members. At the funeral, he announced that he was going to take future profits from that store over a certain time period and donate them to start a fund locally to help this man's family and those in similar circumstances. He is all about the values; he decided he would not send an emissary, but go himself and comfort the family. When I told this story at a Disney leadership conference, the best friend of that man's sister waited afterward to tell me the rest of the story. Every year that has passed, on the anniversary of his death, flowers arrive for the family and the store. There is no card with them, but everyone is certain they are from Howard Schultz.

Rick Kelleher, former CEO of Doubletree Hotels and currently CEO of Pyramid Hotels in Boston, advocates taking your values out for a walk, too. In his opinion, leaders must be as concerned about the communities they operate in as they are with the day-to-day business of their organizations. This goes far beyond writing checks to charities; you have to get involved personally. Kelleher and his wife devote much of their time to an inner-city boys' middle school in Boston, in a neighborhood where many of the company's employees live. Kelleher would undoubtedly be involved in the community whether or not he was trying to live Pyramid's value of commitment. But he also realizes that being seen living the values—and encouraging employees to get involved in the community—helps reinforce the values. "Leadership is actions and deeds done in a humble way," says Kelleher. "Be a servant and help other people achieve their goals and dreams."[7]

Through the company's Care Committee, Pyramid employees are helped to contribute to their communities, as they wish, in their off time. The committee also recommended that the company offer to match employee contributions to Haiti relief, and raised $100,000 in a very short time. "A Care Committee at each property ensures that employees feel that we respect their communities," says Kelleher. "This is the way a business lives—a set of values that reach down through our whole organization." The leadership team can also reinforce the best behaviors by holding each other accountable, just as they would for front-line employees.[8] On the other hand, expecting employees to display behaviors that you do not demonstrate is the fastest way to fuel cynicism and turn your values effort to dust.

CELEBRATE SUCCESS

Leaders seldom spend enough time savoring success themselves, let alone helping their people to do so. But that is just what is necessary to build a strong culture on values. When your employees have made a strong effort to do something well (such as developing the Values Blueprint!), find a milestone to celebrate, in person. No, it doesn't have to be a goofy thing (like Herb Kelleher barbequing on the tarmac in a ladies' robe and hair curlers) if that is not your organization's style. The point is to make sure your employees feel like their efforts are being recognized. And there are a few ways to do it that can easily be worked into an organization's daily operations, which make it easier to recognize and reward successes.

JetBlue was awarded the J.D. Power Award for best customer service in the low-cost airline category in 2010. It was the airline's sixth consecutive win in just ten years of its existence. CEO Barger immediately sent out a celebratory Blue Note to every employee. "Dear Crewmembers, You've done it again—simply outstanding!" He went on to give the details of their metric of 764 out of a 1,000-point scale that measures customer satisfaction in seven categories and compared it to other airlines. "An amazing feat," he said, while announcing that, "to celebrate in style," he'd be taking the trophy on a tour of all of JetBlue's sixty-three stations. "I have to believe this decade will be even more rewarding thanks to our most important asset—YOU—and our focus on making the JetBlue Experience even better." It's signed "Dave."

Seems like a minor thing to send a regular personal e-mail to all employees. You probably do it yourself. The trick to celebrating success, though, is to touch employees with the values across multiple platforms, without making it seem like you are trying to create some kind of phony cheerleading squad. An effective leadership communication program informs, rewards, listens, and also celebrates across multiple platforms—e-mail, podcast, broadcast, and handwritten notes.

An important part of celebrating success is the personal touch. Catch someone behaving the right way in your presence, and it's easy to reward them with praise. But what of employees (the majority) who exhibit excellent behaviors far from your sight? You need to have systems in place that make it easy to deliver personal rewards from leaders without making them robotic. A well-designed communications system will allow you or your outreach team to personalize quick notes and rewards. Make sure all communications come from your heart and reflect your true feelings about the company and its values. All that is required is a commitment from you to send them out on a timely basis. This allows top leaders to be "on the ground" even when they are thousands of miles away.

Both Southwest and JetBlue have a system of "story telling" that allows employees and managers to solicit or receive top management recognition for living the values. One person in communications is responsible for forwarding success stories illustrating the values or great customer service stories of any kind (which also show the values) found in customer e-mails or from peers directly to the CEO and department heads. A personal letter, e-mail, or certificate is generated over the CEO's signature to say thank you. Big deal? It is a big deal when those letters are sent by mail to employees' homes. Nearly always, the employee who receives one of those letters brings it back to work. So we get a two-for-one, multiplying the praise both within the family and among coworkers. In fact, I have received several certificates as a JetBlue director after interactions with customers that have been recognized, and they are sent to my home, too.

In difficult times, having these systems in place becomes even more important. When you're downsizing or facing troubles of any kind, the temptation is to hide, which worries everyone even more. Instead, you need to personally communicate the positives and negatives so that your people will trust that you have the situation in hand. The strongest indicator of a values-rich company is hearing the leaders admitting mistakes when they happen and saying you are doing your personal best to solve them. You'll do this if you want to retain those A Players you worked so hard to hire. Know this: once trust is lost, regaining it takes a lot of years.

DO THE SMALL THINGS RIGHT

You are being watched. The smallest move you make at work is observed by someone in your organization; every communication is analyzed. The juiciest ones end up on the office grapevine, fodder for lunch table discussion. That's an accepted part of leadership and something that you probably don't think about much. And that's a mistake. Your words and actions are vital components in determining the success or failure of your values culture. You can either undermine that developing culture through actions that are contrary to it or reinforce it by taking advantage of the fact that people are watching you.

Think twice about the privileges of leadership. In my experience, employees who feel that their leadership team is flaunting their status will be significantly less motivated to make the effort to uphold values-laden behaviors. Changing your culture from "my company" to "our company," on the other hand, will make a big difference.

Action Step 4: Live the values you want people to emulate

If your values are important to you, you'll show it in both big and small ways. Yet it is the small things leaders do that have the greatest impact on the visuals, and what people actually witness leaders doing creates a stronger and longer lasting impression than the things they hear. Here are some small things you can do to show that you are committed to living the values:

- Let your top people take the hit first if salaries or benefits must be reduced in difficult times. Layoffs? There had better be some in the executive suite as well if your values are going to survive the downtimes.

People who are still employed by you after the cuts are going to be acutely aware of how you have handled it.

- Ditto the expense account. Think about what your executives (and you) are spending company money on. Once accounting gets the bill, word will get around if something is outlandish. One company executive was going to put me up in a private club when he asked me to consult with him about cutting his nursing staff. I politely declined.
- Have a sense of fun about yourself. Even if fun is not one of your values, people want to know that you don't take yourself too seriously. Being able to make jokes at your own expense puts people at ease, especially front-line employees and new hires.
- Give up on perfection, for everyone. Encourage your people and yourself to experiment and try new ideas. Things won't always go as planned, although you can expect more successful outcomes than unsuccessful ones from motivated people. Make sure your people, even at the front-line level, have the authority to be flexible as long as safety is not compromised. And be sure to refrain from immediately expressing your opinion about why something won't work and to concentrate on the positives.
- Be consistent about on-the-spot recognition, and constantly tell stories about employees living the values. Telling stories may feel uncomfortable for some executives—particularly repeating the same story for different audiences. To maintain a good supply of new stories and to stay excited, it is important to always be on the lookout for outstanding employee behaviors to reward and recognize on the spot. Keep track of these and you'll always have a fresh supply of stories to tell about employees living the values. Upshot: nobody's bored, and people feel celebrated.

At the end of the day, the great cultures pay attention to both the large and small things. Here's what I have learned: If you can get the small things right, the large things become a lot easier.

REWARD THE VALUES IN THE C-SUITE

Leaders must model the values and behavior they want to see in employees and create systems to reinforce that behavior. At JetBlue, executive performance reviews are set up to reinforce values and behaviors, just as they are for the rest of our "crew members." We get feedback from people who report to the leaders and, for the CEO, from the entire board. All others in the executive suite get "320" reviews (equivalent to a 360 review, and a play on words honoring the aircraft we fly, the Airbus 320). Many other high-performing companies, including eBay under Meg Whitman and Starbucks under Howard Schultz, operate under the notion that executives should be held to the values and behaviors required of all other employees. Everyone at Loma Linda University Medical Center, too, is subject to this same sort of performance evaluation, starting at the top with CEO Ruthita Fike. In fact, all of our clients have put some version of values-based executive review in place. This is one of the reinforcing factors that help companies, even small ones and nonprofits, create what *Inc.* magazine calls "workforces whose productivity is born of passion, whose loyalty springs from the perception of beneficence and fair play."[9] Fair play is something you can't fake. It needs to start with you.

As a result, performance reviews on the values and behaviors must have consequences at the top, as well. At JetBlue, bonuses in the C-suite are based on the company's overall net promoter score—its measure of customer and employee satisfaction derived from random surveys. One year the employee satisfaction score dipped. Bonuses at the top reflected that, and executives got busy making changes the employees wanted. The problem was solved fairly quickly, and net promoter scores rose once again. Everyone was happier. It was a great "living the values" outcome.

Total rewards in the C-suite should, in fact, be tied as much as possible to the behavior-based metrics—compensation, bonuses, and stock options. At JetBlue all executive salaries are tied to performance metrics—and we didn't get a single complaint at the shareholders' meeting about "say on pay." It just didn't come up. We make the connection to performance clear. If total rewards are tied to actual metrics, everyone will be happier.

Some executives, of course, are not motivated by compensation. Some of the leaders I most admire have been paid, at some point in their careers, at or below market and yet the media would have us believe that all executives are paid far above the market. The compensation committee at P.F. Chang's China Bistro spent years asking Rick Federico to make his salary more market competitive, and until recently he refused. He and his co-CEO have also on occasion distributed a portion of their stock options in order to make sure others were adequately rewarded. Just as you would for front-line employees, you should question your leadership team about what motivates them and give them more of that when their behaviors support the values.

Some values-rich executives I have had the pleasure of working with were known for giving part of their compensation away. Make sure your organization gives them opportunities to do this and be recognized for it. The JetBlue Crewmember Crisis Fund (JCCF) has received many donations from executives wanting to help crew members with financial problems. The fund now has more than $3 million invested and gave away a half million in the first six months of 2010 alone. Such behavior has inspired employees throughout the organization to contribute generously to the fund as well, through optional pay period donations.

NEVER LOSE AN A PLAYER

Finally, if you want to fill your company with A Players, you need to prevent the ones you have from leaving. It goes without saying that you'll reward them well, compensate them competitively, develop their talents, and inspire them to believe in the values. The other method: never take a "permanent" resignation from an A Player. At JetBlue we had what could be called a rapid response team for resignations. Whenever we learned that a good player was about to resign, a senior officer—many times, the CEO—would immediately go into action, even if one of us had to get on a flight and go to another city. Because so few good employees voluntarily leave JetBlue anymore, we wanted to talk to any great employee on the verge of resigning and find out what the problem was. We were interested in asking why the employee wanted to leave us and in changing the situation if possible.

Of course, you can't do much when employees leave because of a job change by a family member or another reason beyond your control. Or can you? I learned from one of my mentors that it is *never* necessary to lose an A Player. Years ago, when I worked for First Interstate Bank, my husband's job was taking him to Dallas, where there were no First Interstate locations. The CEO didn't want to lose me, so he went so far as to recruit my husband to work at the bank so we wouldn't have to move. Even though that didn't happen, he stayed in touch with me for twenty years, always calling me on September 20, which he believed was my birthday. Before he retired, we worked together on two more projects when he felt he could use my experience and ideas. In all those years, I never had the heart to tell him that my birthday was actually November 20!

I did the same thing when I started my company. I had kept in touch with the people I knew I would want to work with again in my lifetime. When I called them, they all said, yes, they would love to come and work for my company. Many times, people who leave you will find the first opportunity to return if you make it clear that you are not really accepting their resignation. And over the years I have had a number of players return to my organizations because I have stated in touch. All my favorite CEOs take the time to get to know their A Players at all levels in the company and keep them on the team, if at all possible. And it's usually possible.

Leaders are the key to the success of a culture built on values. Every action they undertake needs to be considered in light of its potential impact on that culture, even seemingly small, everyday decisions, like where to stay on trips and what kind of transportation to use. What kind of message will these decisions send about your commitment to the values culture? A conscious effort must also be made to devote leadership resources to building the culture. It takes time to listen to people, be open to feedback, tell stories, and celebrate successes. But, guess what? That's part of your job, if you want this to succeed. Do you need to devote 50 percent of your time to it, like Dave Barger does? Perhaps not. If you are thinking, though, that you can't possibly squeeze any more into your day, think about how much time you spend thinking up and discussing solutions for problems in employee turnover, customer service, and bottom-line performance. Just think of it as solving these problems a different way, a hands-on way. Isn't that what you became a leader to do?

CHAPTER 8

REINFORCE YOUR VALUES CULTURE

Be Excessive About Communication

The success of the Values Blueprint and culture change rests on how well the values are integrated into the organization, and a major part of integration is effectively communicating the meaning of those values to both employees and customers. There is an observable difference in the quality of customer loyalty, and thus the bottom-line results, between companies who make communication of values to both employees and customers a priority and those who believe it will take care of itself. Most tellingly, the most effective communications of values go far beyond just words on paper.

The best employees in a values-centric culture, who have come to embody the values in a fundamental way, will communicate those values unconsciously to other employees and to customers. Eventually you will develop a self-reinforcing level of communications about values at which they become second nature to your organization. The values you have chosen then become who you are and what you communicate every day.

In the meantime, conscious, repeated efforts at communication are required to reinforce the values and behaviors of your Values Blueprint to ensure that they permeate the organization. For that reason, in my opinion, developing a comprehensive plan to communicate the values is just as important as the Blueprint itself. The Values Team, which was responsible for setting the values at the Values Workout in the first place, needs to build support for the values throughout the organization by developing and implementing a values communication strategy, typically in conjunction with corporate communications and marketing people. Priority must be given constant communication both top down and bottom up, using your values to rebrand your company, giving authority at all levels to actions that reinforce the values, and listening for feedback for ways that communication needs to be improved.

You cannot force culture; you can only create the environment. Constant communication of the values, in all directions and with creative methods, is the only way to ensure the fierce customer loyalty that is the hallmark of solid long-term performance. Traditionally, corporate communications has been thought of as an information transmittal function, often from the top down to the employees and from the organization to its customers. Communications that create a desire to exceed customer expectations are more all-inclusive, as strong from the bottom as from the top, as strong from the customers as toward them.

If you build your culture around customer-oriented values and A Players, you will exceed the expectations of your customers every day. A 360 strategic communications plan based on values simply allows you to astonish them on a more consistent basis. Executives, particularly in the communications area, can develop ideas for these communications paths but not dominate or control them. At best, they should emphasize and model creative communications in multiple tangible and intangible ways, while empowering employees and front-line supervisors with the authority to select (or create) the methods they deem best. That includes giving customers the benefit of the doubt, which is also a way of communicating your values, loud and clear. If a good customer's daughter presents a gift certificate allegedly from him, would you want the front-desk employee to refuse to cash the certificate if it looks a little funny, or would you want that employee to call the good customer to verify the purchase—and believe him when he did? The answer will be obvious on the front line only if you've conveyed that treating customers well (whatever the name of the value that gets this across) is part of your culture.

The good news is that all of the effort to communicate the values effectively pays off, in a measurable way. A 2009 report by Towers Watson, a global HR consulting firm of 328 organizations and five million employees worldwide, found that those with the most comprehensive communication efforts ("high-effectiveness companies") had a 47 percent higher total return to shareholders over five years than firms with the least comprehensive communications. "In times of change," note the study's authors, "[successful companies] use social media and other time-tested tools to communicate to an increasingly diverse and dispersed audience . . . They focus on the customer and use communication programs to drive productivity, quality and safety."[1]

The ideal is to create a high-touch culture with much more buzz going on—inside and out—than you may think is strictly necessary. Young employees, especially, have grown up in a world of constant multidirectional communication where even momentary silence signals indifference. "Once you think you are communicating enough, step back and triple your effort," says Dave Barger, CEO of JetBlue Airways. "People forget, they go back to old habits, new people are hired. You especially can't lose sight of the importance of communication with mid-level supervisors, which can be an Achilles heel for many organizations. You need to keep those supervisors aligned with the values."[2]

COMMUNICATE UP, DOWN, AND BACKWARDS

Our employees want more information than we think they do. Our customers, especially those experiencing difficulties with us, want even more. In the absence of good communications, people will listen to whomever is talking the loudest. Leaders, of course, have to get lots of earnest communications out there on a regular basis. But a huge amount of information dissemination must go on outside the executive suite as well, although—and this is key—it cannot be perceived as a huge amount of information. Methods like workgroup dashboards are a good start and a good model for other communications. If you think you can't convey it quickly in a dashboard or scorecard format, why not? Can you tweet it? Maybe you can't pare some information down so thoroughly, but short and concise should be your guiding principle. We can learn a lot from modern media. If a proposed communication takes a college degree and a half day to figure it out, you can forget it. You know that while your employees may have the college degree, they won't give you the half day (or even a half hour). When you give people a complicated report to comprehend, you are communicating that you don't value their time. Habitual or easy for you doesn't make it effective communication. All areas of the company must be involved in creating the Values Communication Plan, an effort that can be led by your Values Team and should involve A Player representatives from the corporate communications and marketing departments, along with selected leaders and A Player front-line people.

There are several key action steps involved in creating a Values Communications Plan. It lays out step-by-step how you are going to communicate the agreed-upon values and behaviors to employees in the most effective way for your company. An effective organizational communication strategy, built most effectively with the help of committed professionals in the corporate communications and marketing departments, engages employees at all levels and encourages support of the process. The Values Communication Plan should include communication methods, timeline, budget, resources, target audiences, and the people responsible for specific communications actions.

A template for a comprehensive values communication plan can be found in the Leader's Toolbox.

Action Step 1: Develop a set of key messages

These are messages about values that will be used consistently in all communications. The key messages will differ for each organization, but the best messages should do all of the following:

- Link the core values to the organization's historic mission and vision. People feel more comfortable knowing how this new focus relates to what has come before.
- Explain the inclusive, participatory process that was used to select the core values.
- Explain the values and their definitions and show the relationship between values and desired future behaviors.
- Present how all of this will affect practical people processes like recruitment, hiring, and, most compelling to current employees, annual review, recognition, and rewards.

Key messages allow you to communicate about the values in a clear and concise way because you are not confusing the audience with conflicting messages. Once you develop a key messages document, make it a part of your Communications Plan and always incorporate the messages into new communications. Your words can be different, but the underlying message thrust should never vary.

Action Step 2: Get commitment from senior leadership and the board

We recommend that the Values Team leader hold one-on-one meetings with each of the key senior leaders to gain their commitment to the key messages. The purpose of these meetings is to get commitment from the executive team to include the values in senior leadership decisions and their own performance evaluations going forward. Most important, senior leaders need to understand their role in developing and communicating the values and leading by example. The Values Team leader should also meet with the board on a quarterly basis to discuss opportunities to build board decisions around the values. These commitments should be expediently communicated in all directions, as well.

Action Step 3: Cascade to operations, staff, and the front line

To be successful at creating a values-rich culture, division leaders and, if applicable, union leadership also need to make a commitment to incorporate the values into operating policies and work rules. And that means that a lot of their internal communications, both written and in person, will need to change as well. The Values Communication Plan should include an examination of communications throughout the operating divisions, including leadership development programs. At JetBlue, we incorporate the values into the entire set of leadership practices that is taught in new leader training; all leaders are expected to operate according to these practices. This cascades down through the organization, as each manager then communicates with direct reports who pass the word to supervisors who continually reinforce awareness of the values and key messages to front-line staff. This process adds credibility to the information and helps front-line supervisors own the values and behaviors.

Action Step 4: Anticipate and minimize resistance

Corporate communications and marketing have vital roles to play in the implementation of the Values Blueprint and its continual reinforcement. When the Blueprint is new, leaders can manage the change better by anticipating resistance and by including a plan to overcome resistance in the Values Communication Strategy. When planning internal and external communications, you can minimize the pushback by taking these actions:

- *Encouraging strong employee involvement in communications.* Employees who are involved in the assessment, planning, and implementation of the Values Blueprint will become natural ambassadors for its success. Plan to use their stories (even let them write some if they wish) to convey what the process involves, including onboarding, hiring practices, and performance evaluation and metrics. Be creative about getting people involved: start a contest to get people to submit their stories online or to call HR with their stories. The more employees see their stories in print, the more it will create a level of energy about finding new stories. At Loma Linda and P.F. Chang's, communications now receives so many stories that they are almost overwhelmed.

- *Making values a regular part of meetings.* At every meeting, make sure that stories are told about people living the values and that employees are celebrated for embodying them. Highlight "values stars" by recognizing them both informally—through a personal e-mail or work group drop-in, perhaps—and formally, with a letter from the CEO or a small reward, as soon as possible after their achievement.
- *Communicating frequently.* Don't assume that once you announce the Values Blueprint or any of its components that everyone will get it. The message needs to be communicated frequently and in a variety of ways to ensure that each employee hears about the new programs. Pick and choose what needs to be sent in company-wide e-mails—don't let the values become spam. Customers, too, should start to hear about it through brand advertising and promotions on social media and at every possible contact point.

In other words, make sure that everyone hears about employees successfully living the values at every opportunity, primarily from their peers. Giving the values message to people with personal credibility among their fellow employees is a particularly effective way to get the message out. Just getting employees talking about the values is a start toward branding your organization as a place where certain values matter very much. You will also want to engage in a formal process of values rebranding.

VALUES REBRANDING

An enormous part of the way you communicate both internally and externally is through your branding. The Values Blueprint, at its most fundamental, is a rebranding effort. Your values are your brand, and the words you use to communicate those values will solidify them in the minds of both employees and customers, so you must be consistent in language and presentation. Because the core values of your organization are now different from what they were, the language you use to communicate what your company is about will also be very different. And, as with any branding or rebranding effort, you must carefully consider the audience.

Strategic plans in both corporate communications and marketing will need to be refocused on values because they must be reflected in every word that comes out of the organization. In Chapter Three I talked a little about the importance of including the best players from both of these areas on your Values Committee and Values Workout Team, and this is when it becomes very important. Your communications and marketing people can help you wordsmith the values, behaviors, and stories about them, which will be a big part of updating your brand. Values that sound fine in one organization will clang harshly in the ears at another, simply because they do not reflect the way your organization uses language. For example, P.F. Chang's embraces the touchstone of candor, while JetBlue's employees launch the value of fun. Just that subtle difference is going to make a huge difference in your rebranding. Tone is everything in reinforcing values—something your best communicators understand.

Effectively communicating your new values plan and the rebranding effort that goes along with that requires a focus that goes beyond ordinary marketing and PR efforts. Sometimes we only talk about our products and services in marketing or PR. Just always remember to keep values in mind as you plan your campaigns to reach out to customers and employees. Here are some additional ways to leverage marketing and PR to communicate your values:

- *Determine how your new values will be incorporated into responses to positive and negative events.* Take the time to incorporate values into your plans for crisis response specifically. Who will be responsible for crafting those values-rich messages, even those that go out over the signatures of the leaders? How will they change or remain the same in response to a crisis? If a company's brand includes the value of aggressive marketing, they might run feel-good ads even in the face of an ecological disaster. But that is not a good response to plan on making, if you want your customers to see your values come to the forefront in a bad situation. Choose the communicators most committed and enthusiastic about the Values Blueprint for this task, so that even in a crisis your communications will be in line with your values.
- *Decide how often you will provide formal values communications.* Communicating too much about values is almost as bad as communicating too little. Daily reminders about the values will soon fade into the wallpaper, and quarterly communications might make the values themselves fade into oblivion. Direct your marketing and PR teams to decide who will communicate with employees about values, behaviors, and celebrations and under what circumstances. Remember, you're communicating not just to make people aware of your brand, but also to make them believe in it. Are regularly scheduled communications right for you? Or would it seem more sincere to establish guidelines for determining what needs to be put before employees? We recommend the latter.
- *Make traditional communication come alive with stories.* Your traditional methods of communication should always incorporate the values and behaviors. This does not always have to be direct and overt: "Here are our values," once again, ad infinitum. But every word your organization utters from now on, internally and externally, should be vetted for adherence to the new brand. That goes double for anything appearing

over a leader's name. Any formal means of communications—intranet news page, newsletters, customer advertising—is a good place to show the new values and behaviors in action. Telling stories about who has been seen living the values and the positive results associated with them is an excellent contribution to rebranding. Continually communicate to employees that the organization is looking for stories to celebrate. Nothing conveys the true meaning of your values more than showing them in action.

- *Use social media to reinforce your brand.* Companies considered less effective communicators were 50 percent less likely to use social media, according to the 2009 Towers Watson study.[3] Even more telling, customer powerhouses JetBlue and Southwest make extensive use of these tools. Southwest assigns five people to be devoted exclusively to its Twitter page and Facebook fan page. "I would say it is a large part of our customer communication strategy," said Christi Day, the airline's emerging-media strategy specialist, in May 2010. (Even creating a job like that speaks volumes about the importance of all-around communications at Southwest.) Day notes that both complaints and kudos are responded to, immediately if possible.[4] Social media outlets also are effective places to encourage employees to post about their jobs. Make sure your communications people, in particular, talk about values whenever they can in social media postings. Younger employees will understand that they count if you reach out to them where they live and you let them reach back.
- *Give priority to communicating your rewards.* After values and behaviors, the most important component of the Values Blueprint to convey coherently is rewards. It is your rewards system that is driving the behaviors associated with your rebranding and your new values, but even the most successful pay and benefits design efforts can be undermined by an ineffective communication effort. In the case of base pay, especially variable pay, the desired behavior changes cannot occur if the participants don't have good information and clearly understand how their efforts can impact business results. Because the design team for rewards

will include people from all levels of the organization, letting them present the new program themselves is the strongest thing you can do to show that people at all levels of the organization will now be rewarded for their values. Use it as an opportunity to generate some excitement about the fact that people are now going to be compensated for living the organizational values as well as demonstrating their skills.

- *Examine "touchpoints."* The Communications Team should make sure that whenever and wherever a customer, prospective customer, employee, or supplier touches the organization, the new brand and values shine through. The Loma Linda Values Recognition Program poster (see Figure 8.1) recognizes these touchpoints specifically. They should even be part of your employee application process and customer service feedback forms. Sit in the employee's or customer's chair for a while. If your values include "caring," do you make it easy on your website for a customer to figure out how to talk to a live person? If not, then you don't really care. Suppliers, too, should be made aware of how important your values are to your organization. When JetBlue outsourced skycap services, we made sure to communicate values and expected behaviors and told them we required that they hold their company's employees responsible for those behaviors while working at our locations. No exceptions. This can be part of the contract or the evaluation of third-party suppliers so that they are aware of these expectations around behaviors.
- *Bring your brand to the family.* The most powerful way to cement a message is to send it home so that families can become reinforcers. Loma Linda University Medical Center engaged in this when they sent their original values DVD to each employee's home with a bag of microwave popcorn and a suggestion to watch it together as a family. New employees should receive the same thing ahead of their first day, too, for viewing at home. Families should also, without question, be involved in as many employee recognition celebrations as possible.
- *Love them when they leave.* In values-rich companies, departing employees are seen as nothing less than potential customers and brand

Figure 8.1. Loma Linda Values Recognition Program Poster

advocates. You can easily spoil a future buying relationship by treating employees less than respectfully when they leave, either voluntarily or involuntarily. You cannot neglect security concerns, but neither should you treat departing employees like criminals, unless they have actually committed a crime and are being led off in handcuffs. Maintaining good will to the very end is key to encourage employees to be net promoters rather than detractors after they leave your employ. Good separation practices must be seen as a values touchpoint, not a throwaway.

- *Use every opportunity to reinforce the brand.* At Redfin.com, a $20 million online real estate brokerage, all executives and product managers are expected to review the values with employees, even if they are there to train people on new technology tools. "There are no scripts," says CEO Glenn Kelman. "We just talk about the values every time we get together. Our people call out things they don't like or question a situation where we might have done things another way. For instance, if we need revenue and there's a house not quite right for a client, do you push it? Not if we want to stick to our values. We find role-playing in those situations to be very helpful."[5]
- *Escalate the sophistication over time.* Everyone must understand that there are phases in the adoption of a new culture. In the beginning, it is all about awareness—getting the values into everyone's brains. The second, and permanent, phase is integrating the values into the soul of the organization. By the second phase, most employees will have tightly integrated the values into their way of operating, and communications will need to reflect that sophistication. New employees in your company therefore will not be appropriate to produce communications materials until they are steeped in the values branding. Communications, over time, must reflect the growing familiarity your people have with the values and their application. To do otherwise will leave your employees feeling talked down to and patronized. As more and more people buy into the rebranding, you can begin to speak more in "values code" in your internal marketing communications because you'll hear it that way in the hallways. In one company, I often hear: "That's very PHISDO

of you"—using an acronym that is now shorthand for the values in the Blueprint. Lots of employees say this—and its opposite—to their managers, all with a sense of humor. Someone with great experience in values communication should be in charge of monitoring all communications for adherence to the rebranding.

Rolling out the brand is equally as important as creating it. The way you conduct your original Values Rollout should be carefully calibrated to fit the personality of your organization. Using a cartoon frog to introduce and reinforce your brand, like Zappos.com does, would be dismissed as unbearably condescending in a company with a more serious culture, like an engineering firm. Implementation strategies, in fact, range along a continuum from organic and gradual to a big bang. On the subtle end of the spectrum, Loma Linda University Medical Center gradually introduced its new values and behaviors across its many locations and departments without overt celebrations, but with a concerted effort to train leaders and supervisors to communicate the values through role modeling and incorporate the behaviors into hiring and rewards.

Other organizations believe their values and marketing strategies point in the direction of a big bang implementation. An organization that needs to present a consistent brand image with customers across a wide variety of locations, for example, might want to opt for big splash that will spread the word about the Values Blueprint strongly and quickly. It makes sense for many small organizations to do it this way, too. Colored T-shirts or buttons for each value and other tangible tokens, perhaps for informally rewarding employees for showing the behaviors, will demonstrate that change has come in a big way. Plus, distributing "things" associated with the values will have the added benefit of sparking questions among customers and vendors. Getting your people to understand and explain to others the idea that "you are on the outside what you are on the inside" disseminates the concepts all the faster. Rapid rollouts also require leaders to travel extensively and communicate intensely about values through town halls, conference calls, and podcasts. The only drawback of a rapid rollout comes if your organization has introduced numerous programs in the past with a big bang that ended up going nowhere. You might be best served by a quieter rollout in that case, to be more believable simply by contrast.

Juniper Networks ended up choosing the rapid rollout by introducing values through its powerful "Trio Tours," in which the values and behaviors were introduced in low-key sessions worldwide conducted by teams of three leaders from the C-suite. No T-shirts or trinkets, but lots of talking and answering questions about values, metrics, and implementation during an intense worldwide introduction over a two-month period. It was just the kind of analytical method suited to the comfort level of a bunch of engineers.[6]

Timeline and strategic communication planning for reinforcing the values must take these different corporate personalities into account as well. Otherwise, implementation problems are almost certain to arise.

How can you tell if your rebranding effort hasn't been so successful and the values are going off the rails in your organization? If you set up listening sessions or pocket sessions, as suggested earlier, you will be far ahead in recognizing signs of communications breakdown early. Early warning signs of such problems include the following:

- *Values being used as a weapon.* "Mary is so horrible at being caring," for instance. What should be a fine tool of guidance to help people improve their results is instead used as a cudgel.
- *Rampant rumors.* Slack off on the values or start withholding information, and you will also find that rumors become a problem. The rumor mill is always operating; you will never eliminate it. Your job is to feed the people at the center of the rumor mill with better information than they will get anywhere else. These are the opinion leaders that your people listen to; supervisors know who they are. With visible metrics and great transparency about plans on the part of leaders, there should not be a lot of negativity circulating on the office grapevine. Take the extra step

and visit the lunchrooms, take opinion leaders on site visits, invite them to e-mail you. If left to their own devices, they will make things up.

- *Apparent silo building.* If information gets stuck in certain departments or disappears into middle management, this can be a significant barrier to Values Blueprint implementation. You want all leaders to be messaging about the brand the same way, and corporate communications can help significantly in the effort. But if department leaders just want to be left alone in their old ways, upper management will have to find a way to coach them into new ways of thinking or terminate them respectfully. If a leader is building silos, it is a powerful indicator that that person should be encouraged to find new employment, even if you have to send out his or her resume yourself. Investigate the cause of significant quality or service breakdowns, as this could be the source. Finger pointing is an unmistakable sign that silo building is the culprit.
- *Lack of honesty with the press.* If you have significant service breakdowns, as JetBlue had with its Valentine's Day shutdown in 2007—when a plane full of people sat on the tarmac for ten hours—then enforce complete openness with the press, customers, and employees. Your communications plan should be quite adamant that nothing is to be hidden or excused. Your organization will be light years ahead of competitors if you do so. In this twenty-four-hour news cycle media age, your secrets will not stay secret for long anyway. Did British Petroleum do itself any favors in the spring of 2010 by initially minimizing the amount of petroleum that was gushing from their well after the explosion in the Gulf of Mexico? It did not. Did the spectacle of the BP, Halliburton, and Transocean blaming each other for the spill before Congress improve their image with the world? Finger pointing, rather than problem solving, is never the best response to a crisis. JetBlue's response to its Valentine's Day problem (escalating compensation for time spent on the runway, for instance) and daily responses to passengers, on the other hand, has been used as a model for a Passengers' Bill of Rights by Congress.

What you are striving for is to communicate what MIT Sloan School of Management professor Glen L. Urban calls the "trust imperative." According to Urban, organizations can no longer push their products onto customers, but must develop trusting partnerships with them or risk losing them forever. Urban says that "if a company is wrong in obvious ways, then the customer might wonder if the company is wrong in other, more subtle ways. To develop a trust-based relationship with customers, a company must become more transparent to those customers."[7] I agree, 100 percent.

GIVE AUTHORITY TO COMMUNICATE THE VALUES TO CUSTOMERS, THEN ASK FOR SUCCESS STORIES

Giving an employee responsibility without actual authority is the quickest way to frustrate and demoralize that employee. Values-based metrics allow you to modify your customer-management systems to allow frontline people more decision-making authority. If you want to communicate your values, the best way is to give your people the authority to rectify any situation in which the company is obviously in the wrong—and give special service to customers when needed. When it comes to correcting errors and giving memorable service, almost nothing should rise to the level of the executive suite.

At P.F. Chang's, the values (which they call "stones") include both hospitality and passion. Outreach to customers far beyond the call of duty—including surprise parties for customers and send-offs before surgery, often at a discount or free—are applauded and encouraged employee behaviors. This results in both the unspoken communication of the gesture to make customers feel special and the overt communication of sharing praise with everyone in the company. Praise given to one person is appreciated; praise shared with everyone multiplies. The constantly repeated corporate communications strategy to share corporate feedback inspires the feedback loop that you need to make values-laden communications effective.

"Over both our brands [Chang's and Pei Wei] is a simple message: 'We're glad you're here, and we are going to do anything we possibly can to get you to come back,'" Rick Federico, co-CEO of the company, recently told me. "We want to give employees the ability, authority, and responsibility to do that, and then we want to celebrate those stories throughout the organization." Stories that show employees going beyond the call of duty to show hospitality, passion, or any of the other values stones are posted on an internal employee portal and circulated within the brand through e-mails from the COO, says Federico. "Sharing as liberally as you can allows people to feel comfortable living the culture," he said. "If everybody else is doing it, they want to play, too."[8]

Employees at the P.F. Chang's location in Olathe, Kansas, saw a posting on their Facebook page by a girl named Jennifer who had just had her wisdom teeth removed. Jennifer posted to the Facebook fan page that she was begging her mom for the only thing that would make her feel better: an order of Dan Dan Noodles from Pei Wei, a P.F. Chang's brand. Employees monitoring the Facebook page contacted her and within a day they were at her house (twenty-five minutes away) with noodles, lo mein, and a $10 get-well gift card. Her email of gratitude was distributed far and wide within the company: "I just wanted to give you a huge thank you . . . Seriously, you already had a lifetime customer in me and my friends, but now you will have many more customers I hope will come to you because I am definitely spreading the word about what a wonderful company you guys truly are. I can tell you really care about your customers. . . ."[9] In this situation P.F. Chang's not only communicated to the customer just how important she was to them, but also was able to reinforce the values company-wide by distributing her e-mail.

The employees at P.F. Chang's and Pei Wei are able to wow their customers because they have the authority to give special treatment, free food, and gift cards when they feel it will strengthen a relationship. Employees who are steeped in the values will be eager to please customers in this way if they understand that the company values such gestures. Good communications will reinforce that idea. Of course, walking the fine line between pleasing customers and breaking the bank is something that also must be conveyed. This is the financial rationale for variable pay and profit-sharing plans for front-line employees. When their pay is at stake, their eyes will be on the profit/cost relationship of their generosity. Will this gesture win a loyal customer and add significantly to the bottom line? Or will I just be giving away the store? Motivated employees soon learn to listen for the difference. Stories of cost-effective ways to wow customers are the kind that should be spread all over your organization, by whatever means necessary, especially if it involves turning a negative into a positive.

There is nothing more powerful than a quick apology to get a customer to come back. Too often, though, leaders are advised that admitting any guilt at all opens the way for legal action or bad publicity. Some employees are not given the authority to make things right when errors occur or even to convey anything tangible by way of apology. Those are the organizations we see complained about on the Web or written up in newspaper "What's Your Problem?" columns. None of these things enhance your reputation with customers or your claim to care about them.

We advise our clients to include in their communications plans a range of small items their people are authorized to give away. At Kettering Adventist Health Care in Dayton, Ohio, the nursing team has a box of "ask forgiveness certificates," gift certificates to a wide variety of local retailers. If a special meal is late or a nurse is slow answering a call, for whatever reason, she may give a certificate to the patient. At Florida Hospitals, nurses can give a rose in a bud vase if they want to apologize for something. The point is that it encourages people to say they're sorry right away, when it's most effective.

Of course, robust systems for tracking these valuable monetary communications are key. More than a few customers, when compensated for bad service, will soon figure out something else to complain about, seeking more freebies. A competent authority system will keep track of the name and address of any person receiving compensation and red flag if they try again anywhere in the organization. They will get a call and an apology instead of a monetary dispensation, unless there is evidence that their claim is legitimate (that is, we really did screw up again). Your finance guys might have a blue fit at first at these "giveaways," which is why this kind of thing must be tracked relentlessly. Front-line people must be able to justify their actions, and fail-safes must be employed to keep them from giving away the store to their friends.

ASK, THEN ASK AGAIN

You'll never know what your customers want if you don't ask them. That's why six customers on each and every JetBlue flight randomly receive a short survey. One of the questions always is "What is the one thing you would change about your experience?" In our first year of operation, we received the shock of our lives when many customers said, "Change the coffee." Customer after customer hated the special gourmet coffees we were serving and asked for Dunkin' Donuts brand. We save over six figures in costs every year because our customers told us that.

You may already be surveying customers. But I'll bet anything you are not doing it randomly and immediately after the customer's experience with you. Most businesses have a way of implementing this, though; even restaurants can present it in the context of qualifying for a nice dollars-off certificate. Questions should be carefully fashioned to test whether employees are living up to the values and what the organization can do better next time.

Management also needs to be serious about continually asking employees for their feedback and must be prepared to make the suggested changes, where appropriate. It pays to show your interest in employee opinions. And you should even ask about the effectiveness of communications—a low response rate will give you an indisputable answer. Demonstrate that you are listening, and employees will learn to be thoughtful about their experiences and feed implementable suggestions back to management.

To keep employees interested in listening to customers, leaders need to model that listening behavior to such an extent that lesser leaders can't help but notice. Rick Kelleher, former CEO of Doubletree Hotels and currently chairman and CEO of Pyramid Hotel Group, put it this way: "Our philosophy of communication is to listen twice as much as we talk, for a mutual win-win. My effectiveness is only as good as the people who touch the people who stay in our hotels. But you know, the most surprising thing is to hear that you're *not listening enough.* You need to be constantly challenging yourself to hear what's being said. In our case, we proved that we were listening when we wanted to cut costs by cutting peoples' hours during the recession. They told us loud and clear that they would prefer we cut *jobs* because they needed their forty hours and benefits, as long as we cut people who were not performing. When we proved we were listening by doing just that, our employee surveys actually went up!"[10]

If you think I am overemphasizing the importance of communicating values properly, I assure you, I am not. Overcommunicating with regard to your values is impossible, as long as you define communication as comprehensively as possible. Talk about the values, listen for incongruities, observe behavior, ask for feedback, go out of your way to wow a customer: everyone, from the executive suite to the front line, should be open to receiving information from all these sources. Top it all off with a formal values rebranding effort, and you'll have an organization that communicates what it's really about and can be proud of it. And that is vitally important to creating a competitive edge.

CHAPTER 9

CONTINUOUS DISCIPLINE

Create a Plan for Culture Maintenance

Though they're fun companies, JetBlue and Southwest Airlines are not young companies. How have they kept their caring, fun, safe cultures going for so many years? Their leaders understand that you never "arrive" at an ideal culture. A culture built on values requires continuous discipline. Even if you are happy with the way your people are executing the values and behaviors, you must be constantly vigilant and revisit your progress on a regular basis. Organizations that succeed with culture change over the long term create an intentional plan for continuous improvement. Culture maintenance is as important as culture creation. Just because a process is successful at one point in time does not guarantee success over time.

Your role as a leader is to continue to find ways to improve the customer, client, patient and family, and employee experience, while not letting success go to your head. The minute you become arrogant about your performance is when you become blind to faults in the system. An ongoing effort is required to ensure that the values and behaviors you have identified are fully integrated into your operating systems. It requires collective dedication of resources to keep developing and thriving in the direction you desire.

People do what is "expected and inspected," which is why values-rich organizations carefully reward people for behaving according to the values. With A Players, in particular, you have to keep raising the bar in order to keep their interest and make it worthwhile for them to come to work. More of the same does not move them; performance reviews, even good ones, don't excite them. The J.D. Powers customer service award is an annual goal at JetBlue, with ever more challenging goal posts—simply winning the award is not enough anymore after six straight wins; improving our score has become our continuous improvement goal. The same goes for the rest of our metrics, including the net performer score—the measure we use for employee and customer satisfaction. As the years go by, good is no longer good enough. Our crew members aspire to be great and greater.

Attitudes like that, built firmly into the organization, actually inoculate it against hard times. During the recent recession, continual improvers like P.F. Chang's China Bistro and JetBlue thought of innovative ways to excite their customers into spending more money, instead of just charging more. P.F. Chang's, for instance, introduced a lower-cost prix fixe menu that proved very popular. And believe me, neither JetBlue nor Southwest has ever considered charging for bags; that doesn't accord with the values of either. Far from charging for the privilege of bringing your clothes along on your trip, JetBlue still offers six unlimited complimentary snacks. It also developed an upgraded pillow and blanket that customers could buy and take with them—comfy and more sanitary at the same time. Not surprising that both companies still finish near the top of industry customers service ratings each year.

But even organizations with their hearts in the right place may find that, as challenging as it is to implement their Values Blueprint initially throughout their organization, *continuing to implement it* is the hardest part. Leaders sometimes get very excited about this at the beginning and then lapse back into their old ways. In part, this can be traced back to people who hunker down and pray that this might be a flavor of the month that will go away if they wait long enough. A major thrust of the initial implementation phase must be aimed at convincing people that this is a new way of life, with the full support of leadership, particularly the CEO's. Our new operating instructions, in other words, will be built around the values and behaviors that define us.

Everyone must understand from the beginning that your culture won't change overnight and that this is a permanent change. We have found that if you begin hiring for front-line jobs according to the key attributes you've discovered, and if you get front-line people involved in the Values Blueprint process and interviewing from the beginning, you will see significant changes in your culture pretty quickly. But in the context of culture change, "pretty quickly" is likely to mean six months or more.

Along the way, celebrating even the smallest success through a variety of communications channels helps people refocus and become more committed to seeing it through, even at the executive level. This is particularly the case when turnover metrics and customer service surveys begin to show improvement. And if you are implementing this in a consistent fashion, those statistics will be the first ones to start showing a turnaround.

Your results should improve further as you implement the metrics scorecards and reward for the behaviors throughout the organization. Most organizations find it easiest to introduce behavior-based rewards and performance reviews on a rolling basis starting with the departments that have the most customer contact or greatest impact on performance. That "inspect what you expect" structure immediately impresses on the mind the changes that are going to be necessary on the part of individual employees. The systems we recommend are internally reinforcing so that results appear almost without management effort. And visible results in the departments that implement them first will help spread the good word throughout the organization, leading good employees in other departments to clamor for the privilege of joining the party.

That enthusiasm, in turn, helps make the effort to continuously improve upon the Values Blueprint an easier task. For one thing, once the nay-sayers realize that the values emphasis is not going away, most will quickly self-select out of your organization. Then there are the stubborn hangers-on: you can either show them the door or send their resumes to organizations where their values would fit into the environment better. Everybody will be happier.

One of the beauties of the Values Blueprint process is that blockages are often as readily apparent as successes. For example, if turnover rates are not falling in key departments or if people are still being hired who do not respect your values, you need to inspect the values interviewing process. Possible causes include interviewers not being adequately trained in interviewing for the attributes and values through stories. We find that interviewers, until they are comfortable with the new techniques, tend to accept claims about results ("I increased sales by 30 percent") when they should be digging for stories ("This is how I increased sales by 30 percent"). They could be interviewing so infrequently that they have forgotten what they need to do. Realize that the difficulty could as easily reside with the managers doing the interviewing as with the peer interviewers. In fact, blockages on the interviewing side are likely to be occurring at the management level because many managers have been interviewing a different way for their whole career and find it easier to fall back into old habits. Interviewers need to get refresher training annually and be rewarded for hiring good people who stay over the long term.

You might also be trying to take shortcuts that undercut your values process. Some organizations, for example, decide that every job in the company has the same key attributes ("friendliness," say). Management is, of course, trying to save time and money by not identifying key attributes for each job. But is friendliness really a *key* attribute if the job is to analyze medical tests in a laboratory? Probably much more important would be accuracy and ability to communicate. We would argue that if you spend the time up front determining the attributes of A Players, you will hire better people, improve the quality of your overall workforce, and see your cost per hire decline steeply after the system is in place.

I consider Loma Linda University Medical Center to be the gold standard for values implementation and maintenance; leadership grasped the importance of behavior-based values right away and got behind the process enthusiastically from the beginning. They even created the Mission and Culture department, run by Dr. Gerald Winslow, to place the emphasis on their newly defined culture. Mission and Culture handles all of the human resources work, as well as the living and breathing of the values. Even so, in 2010, three years later, Winslow reported that just 72 percent of his department heads, representing about two hundred departments, were trained on and practicing values interviewing. His goal is 100 percent, and he is likely to achieve it, sooner rather than later. But that three-year timeline is absolutely the average for larger organizations to implement this process from top to bottom. That points to the crucial nature of continuous improvement in departments where your Values Blueprint has already been implemented, while everyone catches up.

CONTINUOUS DISCIPLINE FOR CONTINUOUS IMPROVEMENT

We recommend making an annual review of the Values Blueprint and its component parts as part of your organization's formal year-end planning. The Values Team should lead departments and work groups in a review of their practices. The end result should be action items and goals to be implemented at both the organization and work group levels. The team should first create checklists to help evaluate the extent to which the values have been integrated into the organization and then review the critical success factors in hiring, evaluating, rewarding, metrics, communication, and, yes, executive behavior. Be clear with everyone that the review should present reality as it is found in your organization; otherwise, significant improvement is not possible. Also be sure the Values Team identifies achievements that can be celebrated. Then new goals should be set in each of these areas—goals that encompass both incremental aims and stretch goals that will give people something to reach for. Responsibilities for those leading the charge toward the next level should also be clarified at this time.

It shouldn't take a great deal of time to perform an annual values review—no more than a few weeks to gather the information from departments and work groups and determine progress and gaps. Incorporating this into the annual budget cycle allows any needed expenditures on values implementation to be directly incorporated in budget projections. For instance, based on experience over the past year, has values interviewing increased costs through more time spent interviewing or reduced costs through lower turnover? Your actual experience will inform the answer to this question and others as you budget. The only vital outcome is that you don't underestimate the cost of fully implementing culture change. That has been the cause of many a culture change failure. And no matter what: Hold each other accountable.

Action Step 1: Evaluate the extent to which your values have penetrated your organization's people processes

Building a values-based culture takes time; it helps to understand, on an annual basis, what your progress has been. Although every organization will implement the steps outlined in this book differently, monitoring the penetration of the values is a good first step. Your Values Team can decide what factors need to be included in this review, based on your organization's priorities, but we have found that several common factors are profitable to evaluate. Consider to what extent:

- ❑ Core values are recognized by every department and work group.
- ❑ Core values drive decisions made at all levels.
- ❑ Every employee can state your values from memory.
- ❑ Specific behaviors have been assigned to the core values

- ❏ Behavior-based values are integrated into the hiring process.
- ❏ All workgroups practice behavior-based interviewing.
- ❏ All workgroups practice team-based interviewing with at least three people, including a peer, interviewing all candidates, even executives.
- ❏ All employees who conduct interviews have been trained in behavior-based interviewing skills.
- ❏ Behavior-based values are integrated into the performance review and appraisal process.
- ❏ You make hiring decisions based on your values; all hiring decisions are based on the candidate's ability to demonstrate your core values.
- ❏ All new employees are provided orientation in your core values and understand their responsibility to live the values.
- ❏ You make firing decisions based on your values.
- ❏ You provide recognition and rewards based on the values.

The key is to determine the extent to which you are doing these things organization-wide and set goals aimed at continuous improvement every year. The closer you are to 100 percent implementation, the closer you are to complete integration of the values. And although 100 percent is not realistically possible due to factors such as the need to train new hires, you can get pretty darned close if attention is paid. Action items and responsibilities should be assigned by the Values Team, based on a careful gap analysis. The team should concentrate its efforts (1) where the most significant improvement is possible at the least cost, and (2) where blockages in specific departments and work groups have been identified.

For a list of factors your Values Team should take into account to evaluate implementation progress, see the Values Team Review Checklist in the Leader's Toolbox.

Action Step 2: Make sure your operational metrics support the values

The Values Team should annually or semiannually review the extent to which employee engagement in the business is being fostered and capitalized on by your organization with metrics. Here is a sample checklist with some things to consider when determining whether or not your business operations support your values:

- ❑ We have developed and communicated a simple Organization Dashboard whose metrics are easily understood by all employees and are relevant to support of the values.
- ❑ The Organization Dashboard fits on one clear Microsoft PowerPoint slide, readily accessible to everyone.
- ❑ All workgroups have developed Dashboard metrics and Scorecards with input from front-line employees.
- ❑ Each workgroup has a values champion.
- ❑ Individuals are rewarded based on moving workgroup metrics in a positive direction.
- ❑ There is a clear system for communicating ideas upward.
- ❑ Effective communication vehicles are frequently used to disseminate organizational and workgroup successes to all employees.
- ❑ All employees have access to opportunities to learn about the business.
- ❑ Financial links to performance on the organizational metrics have been established for all employees.
- ❑ Variable pay criteria for employees, where feasible, directly relate to our Dashboard metrics.
- ❑ There are regular celebrations for achievement of goals and metrics.

Your checklist may vary somewhat, depending on the size and maturity of the organization, but you'll need to conduct at least a minimal evaluation of the appropriate items for your organization.

Action Step 3: Review performance expectations, appraisals, and rewards

Behavior-based reward systems are key to mature culture development. As hard as it is for some executives to believe, you get exactly what you reward, every time. Even your entry-level players will develop intense loyalty to your organization when you recognize their effort. JetBlue found that fourteen minutes was the maximum time people would wait for their bags and still rate performance as "good" on surveys. That's a definition of "good" that bag guys understand and will work to achieve, especially if a better performance rating means a better salary and total rewards. Your annual review in this area should look for how much progress your departments and work groups are making in implementing performance-tied appraisal and rewards systems. When evaluating your performance and reward systems, consider the extent to which the following are true:

- ❑ Individual performance expectations are aligned to Dashboard metrics.
- ❑ Performance is appraised based on the values and behaviors of the Values Blueprint.
- ❑ Work groups and individuals are recognized for meeting standards or objectives.
- ❑ Performance appraisals include multi-rater and self input.
- ❑ Behavior-based goals are set every year with each employee's input.
- ❑ Salary, bonus, and incentive decisions are based on performance appraisal results.
- ❑ Promotions and career ladder decisions are based on performance appraisals.
- ❑ Variable pay plans are based on results and perceived as fair and motivational.
- ❑ Traditional benefits plans are perceived as fair and high-quality.
- ❑ Nontraditional benefits plans are perceived as a reward.

These represent the ideal implementation of the Values Blueprint. Some of these won't work for everyone, especially in the early stages, but they should be considered by organizations at some stage in their development as they work toward increasingly high levels of performance.

Action Step 4: Review execution of the values at the C-suite level

Even at the executive level, a visible annual review of their commitment to the values helps keep everyone focused. This level is perhaps most vulnerable to backsliding into old habits simply because the demands on executive time are so great. Tying compensation and rewards at this level to values-based performance at a very early stage in the process is probably the most effective move you can make to concentrate the executive mind on living the values. At JetBlue, values went into the executive performance review from the beginning, and that has made all the difference. No one will deny that it takes courage to take this step; tying your compensation and review to your adherence to values means risking that you may be rated poorly at first and be subjected to lowered compensation. All the more reason for those in the C-suite to pour themselves into the process heart and soul. Fortunately, if you do, the reviews and bonuses will take care of themselves. When gauging C-suite implementation levels, you need to review whether or not:

- ❑ Senior leaders are part of the Values Team.
- ❑ Senior leaders are evaluated by peers and subordinates for adherence to your core values.
- ❑ Compensation and/or rewards of senior leaders depend on adherence to and marketing of your core values.
- ❑ Communications from senior leaders always conform to core values and reinforce them.
- ❑ Senior leaders participate in and encourage the annual review of the Values Blueprint process.

Leaders need to abide by the same behaviors as bag handlers. Top leaders should be evaluated by the board each year, most likely by the compensation committee. I am on that committee for P.F. Chang's and JetBlue, and we give feedback to our CEOs on behaviors and needed changes—and we follow up to see that they happen. Leaders also participate in self-review and peer review. Leaders need to insist that the board hold them accountable for living the values. Taking it a step further, board members must also sit down and think about what they are doing or need to do differently to support the values. This could be part of the annual board self-evaluation recommended by the SEC. A questionnaire can be created to help the board with this self-evaluation. Questions should be specific to your organization's values; for example, if honesty or integrity are one of your values, "Have we represented the shareholders with integrity?" P.F. Chang's even reports the results in our annual board report.

The evaluation the P.F. Chang's board uses to evaluate the CEO each year can be found in the Leader's Toolbox.

Action Step 5: Review and align relationships with contractors, consultants, and third-party vendors

As your organization moves closer to achieving the ideal culture for your values, relationships with outside resources will naturally come under scrutiny. As you create the structures to support your values and increasingly make decisions based on them, it will become obvious which contractors, consultants, and vendors share your values and which do not. Actual malfeasance or dishonesty does not have to be part of the equation; these third parties could be just fine but not right for you. Like C Players, many of them may self-select out of your circle of influence because they may begin feeling as uncomfortable in your new culture as you feel about their values. Others—once again, like C Players—will just put their heads down, do the work you assign them or ship their products to you, and wait for this folly of yours to pass.

An annual review of your third-party suppliers should be encouraged in every department to weed out those who may be, perhaps inadvertently, sabotaging your commitment to your values. A commitment to the value of safety, for instance, could be seriously undermined by temporary contract workers who do not consider that value to be a top priority. Here are some questions to consider in your review:

- ❑ Do all of our third-party vendors, consultants and contractors understand our values and associated behaviors?
- ❑ Do they consistently act on those behaviors in their relationship with us?
- ❑ Are their values, as displayed in our relationships with their employees, a match for our values?
- ❑ Are they willing to make changes to accommodate our Values Blueprint?
- ❑ Do the reasons to continue working with them (for example, they are a low-cost supplier) outweigh our need to live our values every day?
- ❑ Will ending the relationship increase our credibility in the eyes of employees and customers?

Holding third parties accountable for their values is absolutely essential. Encourage your whole staff to regularly monitor their behaviors and report discontinuities they observe, and don't hesitate to fire negative outliers before they do serious damage to your image.

Action Step 6: Be both objective and subjective about getting feedback on your progress

Establish a formalized way of obtaining feedback from customers and employees, such as the net performer score, and compile those measures for use in the annual review process. You may also want to update your baseline appraisal surveys and focus groups that you reviewed at the beginning of the values workout process. Ask the same questions and measure your progress quantitatively. You should also look at the quality of stories that are emerging from your ranks. Are people spontaneously sharing more stories that show people living the values? Are more departments learning to celebrate the achievement of goals and individual performance improvements?

As you evaluate your progress, also ask employees and customers what improvements you still need to make. Management needs to keep its collective mind open about changes that are needed. In addition, you should ask employees to filter their ideas for change thoughtfully through the organization's values and suggest only those that are appropriate for your culture. With a few years of experience under their belts, this will come naturally.

A final surprising thing you may hear in your annual review evaluations: your Values Blueprint itself may need changes. We've found that, once customers and employees have had at least a year's experience with the implementation of your organization's values and behaviors, revision is the norm. Remember this: the Values Blueprint should never be set in stone—or hung up on the wall and forgotten. Your Blueprint is a living document and needs to be regularly challenged against your reality. In business, the competitive environment changes all the time; you can't expect to conquer it with values and behaviors that never change.

STRATEGIC LEADERSHIP DEVELOPMENT AND SUCCESSION PLANNING

The final pieces to the puzzle of continuous culture advancement are strategic leadership development and succession planning. Up-and-coming leaders, thoroughly immersed in and invested in your ideal culture, will keep it thriving for decades to come. Developing those values-rich leaders and enmeshing them in your leadership team must go far beyond typical management training, however. When considering future leaders, you should also think far beyond the typical candidate with an MBA.

There may be a terrific A Player on your front line who would make a wonderful CEO someday because he or she is the perfect exemplification of your values. Open your leadership development programs to anyone who aspires to move up in the organization. Anyone. And let them do it on the clock. That will convince everyone that you are serious that A Players with potential can be found anywhere. Leaders used to start in the mailroom. Who says they can't anymore? Keep your eyes open as you make your rounds, and take names.

A good leadership development program will even help with recruitment and values branding. In a recent study of large company programs, a group of Harvard researchers found that "there is a direct relationship between a strongly defined leadership development program and the type of job candidates the company attracts, external stakeholder's perceptions of the business and employees' understanding of the firm's values and strategies."[1]

Values-based leadership development and succession should allow learning in both business skills and values, in both the workplace and the classroom. The actual shape of it will be determined by what you consider to be the most salient attributes you wish to pass along to people who may succeed you one day. Essential: you cannot just add a "values module" to your existing management development program. Ask your Values Team and HR to completely rethink it: this is where your culture is revealed. Here are some factors we have found essential to include:

1. *Figure out your own personal Values Blueprint and teach it.* Whatever turns you on as a leader needs to be a big part of your leadership development process. "To be inspirational, you need to be inspired yourself," notes Christopher Rice, CEO of BlessingWhite, consultants in employee engagement and leadership development. "Leaders need to articulate goals, paint a compelling vision of the future and help employees connect the dots." White recommends that leaders constantly coach team members to be high-performing leaders at every level, even if the only

ones they are leading are themselves.[2] Inspiring an organization full of committed values coaches is never a bad thing.

2. *Focus far beyond "training."* You cannot train people—even leaders—to have values. Leadership development in sound decision making must now move beyond number crunching and business models. Leaders must have abundant opportunities to learn to make decisions based on values. These could be simulations at first but must eventually move out into the real world. Leaders must deeply understand, before they begin making strategic plays, that even one decision that does not reflect the values can have a huge impact on the success or failure of culture change.

3. *Emphasize communications skills.* Slickness is not required in a values-based organization; believability is. Many executives, even the most sincere, struggle with conveying their commitment to the values when they get in front of groups. In fact, the "best" communicators, pre-Values Blueprint, may be the ones who struggle once values are implemented, as they may have previously relied on prepared, teleprompted remarks that won't fly in the more intimate settings and smaller groups of employees where storytelling skills are required. Coaching and practice in this area should revolve around (a) matching behavior to words so that your behavior reinforces your words; (b) relating to small groups of front-line people as a coworker, not as their superior; (c) conveying common sense and not talking down to people; (d) always having facts and figures at hand, but not being afraid to say "I don't know"; and (e) respecting your audience at all times. Your leaders never have to prove how smart they are, just how passionate they are.

4. *Make values more than just another component of leadership development.* Each component of training must be remade so that the values are incorporated at the cellular level. Each aspect of the training should also be revised to ensure that it reinforces rather than undermines your culture. That goes double for training provided by outside firms, including management training at the university level. A Values Team member, most likely from HR, should take responsibility for vetting and revising leadership development programs with values alignment in mind.

There should also be specific training developed to help leaders and prospective leaders feel comfortable conveying the values to others. It begins with discussion about how they are personally living the values or struggling with them. This exercise lets leaders develop the vocabulary and the behaviors they need to coach their teams. We encourage them to discuss one value and behavior each month in staff meetings and allow employees to discuss situations in which they lived the values (or didn't) themselves. Learning how to show vulnerability—willingness to fail or fall down—is a key factor in developing credibility for the values among the staff. You and your leaders want to engender a realization along the lines of: "Oh my gosh, he's willing to get back up and try again. That must mean this is really important." Get across the idea, any way you can, that this is a process, not a light switch you can flip on and be done with it.

5. *Provide education in the intricacies of your business.* Employees, even those who work the front line, are better positioned to contribute to the financial health of your organization if they know the details of how the business operates. We recommend offering instruction on interpreting basic business reporting and jargon, to demystify business talk and allow employees to build a higher level of trust in the organization. Such knowledge will also allow them to find and suggest efficiencies in their own work surroundings that could save the company a great deal of money or amaze customers.

6. *Teach executives and managers to plan for succession.* Successful transmission of the values and behaviors to the next generation requires systematic succession planning. Eventually, every single executive, manager, and supervisor should have a successor in place. Why is that necessary if every part of your organization is steeped in the values? First, designating people as named successors who cherish the values of your organization conveys the importance of those values in an exceptionally clear way. Want a promotion? Live the values. Second, naming successors allows their leaders to become conscious mentors, conveying their knowledge of how they have integrated the values into their daily lives and decision making. All of the successors should also be invited into leadership development training.

Picking a successor, for leaders at any level, can be psychologically difficult. Suddenly it seems as if there is an expiration date on your forehead and you are on your way out. Leaders must encourage each other to look at the situation differently. If everyone has a successor, then everyone also has someone above them whose job they will eventually take. After some years of mentoring and learning, moving up in progression will feel inevitable. Even the chairman and CEO can start thinking of the next opportunity, which could come in identifying and acquiring businesses compatible with the values and taking the time to smoothly integrate them into the Values Blueprint.

Your stars will thrive, knowing that they have been picked as a successor to a superior. Retaining high-flyers is often a challenge because they don't need a lot of guidance, although if they are not a part of your formal succession planning they will end up feeling ignored instead of engaged. Focus them on the road ahead and give them the mentoring they need to remain motivated. You know who your stars are; let them know, too.

THE STORY OF SUCCESSFUL CULTURE CHANGE

Living the values can become a way of life in your organization with huge benefits. It can simplify decision making, help you hire the best people, help you keep them working for you for years, give you abundant opportunities to astonish customers, and create an unlimited future for your organization. But that is just the beginning. Suddenly it will be very exciting again to go to work every morning. You'll tell each other stories about what a great place you work for. You'll be excited to come to work every day, and you'll do it again, even better this time, because what you are doing is so satisfying. You'll be glad to jump on a plane and go visit every location, because that's where the employees are—and they've got fascinating ideas to share. Every meeting will include stories about people who are living the values, from the executive suite on down.

Doesn't that sound a lot more soul-satisfying than being a place that focuses solely on financial performance? My partner, Charles Denham, M.D., wrote in a recent article for health care leaders promoting patient safety (along with the actor Dennis Quaid, whose twin infants were injured in a medical accident), "If every story has a hero, a victim, a villain, a crisis and a resolution, we want you to see yourself as a hero. It is time to write your own story. Turn that light into heat and focus it on your villain: the villain that protects the status quo—the way we have always done things."[3] This applies equally as well to leaders in every field considering building a culture around values. The process of culture change is within your grasp. It can start now with the simple discipline of identifying the values that drive your organization. It will succeed if those at the top have the determination to make change happen. Your people, your shareholders, and your customers will thank you for it. Wall Street will even approve of your rising performance. So what are you waiting for?

LEADER'S TOOLBOX

CHAPTER 2

2.1. Sample Values Survey Questions

This survey has been used in many of our client organizations to establish a baseline for the importance of values in your organization and to measure gaps between stated values and actual practice. You may use this verbatim or adapt it for your own needs. To the extent possible, it should be collected and compiled anonymously.

TOOLBOX-EXHIBIT 2.1. ORGANIZATIONAL VALUES ASSESSMENT TOOL

ORGANIZATIONAL VALUES

1.1. Does your organization have a set of identified core values?
- Yes
- No
- Unknown

1.2. Do those core values drive the decisions made by the organization at all levels?
- Yes
- No
- Unknown

1.3. Can every employee within the organization state the values from memory?
- Yes
- No
- Unknown

1.4. Has the organization assigned specific behaviors to the values?
- Yes
- No
- Unknown

1.5. Are the values integrated into the hiring process? (Do your interview questions reflect the values you are looking for in your candidates?)
- Yes
- No
- Unknown

1.6. Are the values integrated into the review process? (Do you hold your employees accountable for living the values by making them a part of their performance evaluation?)
- Yes
- No
- Unknown

1.7. **Does your organization hire for values? (Are you willing to hire someone who may not have all of the trainable skills necessary but does exhibit all of the values?)**
- Yes
- No
- Unknown

1.8. **Does your organization fire for values? (Is your organization willing to fire a high-performing employee who does not live by the values created?)**
- Yes
- No
- Unknown

1.9. **Does your organization provide rewards and recognition to employees based on values?**
- Yes
- No
- Unknown

Source: Developed by CareLeaders™

CHAPTER 3

3.1. Sample Values Blueprints

Values Blueprints can be created in nearly any format, according to the needs of your organization. Your Blueprint does not have to enumerate your mission or vision, although it can, as Loma Linda's does. However, an effective Values Blueprint will always tie specific, measurable behaviors to each value so that employees can more easily incorporate the values into their day-to-day work. This also helps create consistency of performance so that both customers and employees understand the expectations about values and behaviors.

Mission

To continue the teaching and healing ministry of Jesus Christ.

Vision

Innovating excellence in Christ-centered health care.

LOMA LINDA UNIVERSITY

MEDICAL CENTER

Values

Compassion Reflecting the love of God through caring, respect, and empathy.

- Identifies with others and listens to understand them.
- Consistently treats others with courtesy, respect, and kindness.
- Exceeds expectations when responding to needs in an effective and timely manner.
- Acknowledges others by name and greets them with eye contact and a smile.
- Anticipates the needs of patients, family members and co-workers.

Integrity Ensuring our actions are consistent with our values.

- Honors the sacred trust of those we serve.
- Builds trust by giving open and honest feedback.
- Actively solicits feedback and willingly accepts responsibility for actions.
- Respects personal dignity and privacy.
- Follows through on commitments and keeps promises.
- Holds self and others accountable for actions and outcomes.

Excellence Providing care that is safe, reliable, efficient, and patient centered.

- Takes all necessary measures to ensure safe patient care.
- Thoughtfully balances the clinical, operational, and financial impact of actions and decisions.
- Challenges the status quo to ensure an exceptional experience for patients and their family members.
- Sets high standards to achieve and support world-class excellence in education and research.
- Partners with physicians and care givers to ensure accurate, honest communication with patients and family members.

Teamwork Collaborating to achieve a shared purpose.

- Demonstrates passion for the team.
- Shares information and creates opportunities for increasing knowledge.
- Recognizes the contributions of others and affirms and celebrates their successes.
- Respects and encourages differing opinions.
- Clearly communicates ideas and collaborates to break down barriers to safe patient-centered care.
- Commits to continuous learning to ensure team strength and retention of the best talent.

Wholeness Embracing a balanced life that integrates mind, body, and spirit.

- Supports the spiritual mission of faith-based health ministry.
- Demonstrates a positive, peaceful, and hopeful attitude.
- Incorporates daily choices that promote physical well being.
- Uses appropriate humor in interactions with others.
- Demonstrates caring to promote a compassionate healing environment for patients, families and caregivers.

A Seventh-day Adventist Institution

Toolbox-Figure 3.1. Loma Linda University Medical Center Values Blueprint

People Ink Values Blueprint

HIGH ENERGY

Focus on the client, not the clock.
Generate and infuse passion for people.
Tenaciously lead the acceleration of performance.

SIMPLISTIC IN SOLUTIONS

Offer simple solutions to improve performance.
Make the complex simple.
Focus on what really matters.

COURAGEOUS

Have the courage to fire ourselves.
Believe that soft skills have hard, bottom-line results.
Tell the truth, even when it's hard.

CREATIVE MINDS

Use all the crayons in the box.
Build and sustain creative environments.

PLAYFUL

Take our jobs seriously but not ourselves.
Believe that if you obey all the rules, you miss all the fun.
Create a fun work environment.

Toolbox-Figure 3.2. People Ink Values Blueprint

ACCION VALUES

PASSION

- Leads with energy, humility, joy and fun.
- Champions ACCION's needs.
- Tenaciously overcomes obstacles.
- Enthusiastically encourages and celebrates the success of all stakeholders.
- Practices random acts of compassion.

PIONEERING SPIRIT

- Actively recognizes and rewards innovation.
- Embraces change with agility and humor.
- Craves learning, from failures as well as successes.
- Inspires others to think outside the box.

- Exemplifies ACCION New Mexico values.
- Builds trust by continually exhibiting honesty and respect.
- Demonstrates personal commitment to organizational transparency.
- Role models initiative, responsiveness and skill in crucial conversations.
- Actively maintains appropriate boundaries and professional relationships.

- Consistently seeks opportunity for improvement.
- Enthusiastically strives to exceed expectations.
- Exercises personal discipline and rigor to achieve outstanding team results.
- Demonstrates extraordinary execution, delivering quality work products that are accurate and on time or ahead of schedule.
- Takes responsibility for personal well-being.

ACCOUNTABILITY

- Holds oneself and others accountable for behavior, actions and results.
- Proactively and appropriately takes responsibility to be informed and inform others.
- Seeks and embraces feedback.
- Owns mistakes and works to carefully and rapidly repair and learn from them.

Toolbox-Figure 3.3. ACCION Values Blueprint

THE JUNIPER WAY

OUR VALUES	DEFINITIONS	BEHAVIORS	
We are **AUTHENTIC**	We are the genuine article–a company of honest individuals who believe extraordinary outcomes are the result of uncommon and inquisitive thinking and open collaboration. We are a company of many individual; always operating as one global company.	• Is self-aware; knows strengths & weaknesses and is willing to admit mistakes and celebrates successes • Demonstrates willingness to be open and transparent • Acknowledges others; giving credit where credit is due	• Seeks to understand and include different perspectives, always acting respectfully embracing diversity in people and ideas. • Demonstrates the courage to stay true to self, taking a tough and principled stand, even when it is unpopular
We are about **TRUST**	We inspire confidence in colleagues, customers and partners by always acting with integrity, fairness, respect and reliability.	• Acts with the highest level on honesty and integrity • Shares agendas and objectives; encouraging feedback and discussing things in an open, collaborative and respectful manner • Takes responsibility and delivers on commitments	• Acts confidently, but never arrogant • Respects decisions and supports them with enthusiasm and follow through • Assumes positive intentions, viewing conflict as an opportunity to find constructive solutions that helps all succeed
We deliver **EXCELLENCE**	We are driven by our craft. We pride ourselves on executional excellence; measurably delivering beyond expectations. Our work ethic seeks perfection as the goal and believes that disciplined, and repeated effort with input from all sides will yield the best results.	• Is systematic and disciplined in their approach to deliver high-quality outcomes • Acts with a sense of urgency • Relentlessly pursues continuous improvement – has no tolerance for compliancy or mediocrity	• Respects and trusts that others will deliver against their roles and responsibilities • Benchmarks and measures the customer and partner experience turning insights into improvements
We pursue **BOLD ASPIRATIONS**	We believe the networked world enables limitless possibilities. We strive to imagine, innovate and create solutions that transform possibilities into realities.	• Seeks out big, bold challenges that are difficult and make a difference that really matters • Challenges current practices and takes calculated risks to achieve breakthrough results • Embraces great ideas no matter where they come from	• Demonstrates exceptional ability to learn new methods and grow from both successes and failures • Life long learners, displaying a sense of curiosity and inquiry, experimenting with better ways – not afraid of trying new things.
We strive to make a **MEANINGFUL DIFFERENCE**	We strive to deliver the greatest net positive impact to our colleagues, customers, partners, and shareholders. We take accountability for driving to a positive purpose. We behave in a balanced, thoughtful manner that considers every aspect and outcome of our business decisions. We operate as responsible corporate citizens.	• Plays to win on behalf of colleagues, customers, partners and shareholders • Proactively seeks to anticipate and understand stakeholder's needs and perspectives	• Considers and balances the short and long term impacts of our decisions on stakeholders • Measures the impact of decisions and constantly applies lessons from failures and successes to do good for all

December 1, 2009

1

JUNIPER NETWORKS

Toolbox-Figure 3.4. Juniper Networks Values Blueprint

Strategic Initiatives

Quality Process
Improves service and removes non-strategic costs

Business Development
Business Growth Opportunities

Professional Development
Growing professional employees

Innovation
Breakthrough Change

Financial Results
Revenue and cost controls

Mission

Honoring your life story today; Preserving it for every tomorrow

Vision

We will be this community's unfailing standard of excellence for families to celebrate, honor and remember the lives of their loved ones, according to their own customs, traditions and beliefs.

Core Competencies

~ Relationships

~ Product and Service Delivery Excellence

Ethics Quick Test

1. Is it legal?
2. Does it comply with FFC values?
3. How would it look on the front page of the newspaper?
4. If you are not sure, ask!

French Values

Communication
~ Always communicates with respect and open mindedness
~ Is honest and transparent in all communications regardless of consequences

Attitude
~ Acts as a servant - has a servant's heart
~ Supports FFC goals as if an owner to protect and sustain our brand

Teamwork
~ Encourages and compliments team members genuinely
~ Understands the business and the importance of a sense of team

Passion
~ Takes the initiative to solve problems
~ Is solution oriented treating problems as opportunities

Integrity
~ Holds self and others accountable for behavior, actions, and outcomes
~ Owns mistakes - doesn't justify wrong actions

Employees
~ Practices Open Door policy
~ Commits to professional development both individually and corporately

Toolbox-Figure 3.5. French Mortuary Values Blueprint

CHAPTER 4

4.1. Conducting Key Attribute Interviews

Here are some tips and talking points you may want to include to brief your key attribute interviewers for values-based behavioral interviews. CarePix is a tool we developed for the health care world; however, the points are easily adaptable to any organization.

CAREPIX KEY ATTRIBUTE INTERVIEWS: TALKING POINTS FOR BRIEFING KEY ATTRIBUTE INTERVIEWERS

The following talking points are used to brief employees who will be conducting Key Attribute interviews:

- CarePix is based on the philosophy that past performance and behaviors will predict future performance and behaviors. If we can determine which behaviors contribute to success in a job, and then interview candidates against those behaviors and values of the organization for a match, we can select better hires for our organization.
- **Types of Key Attributes**
  - Competency-based—attributes that tell us the ability of the candidate.
  - Value-based—attributes that tell us the likes and dislikes of the candidate and whether they will fit the organization's values.
- **The Process**
  - Interview Employees Currently in the Job

    Key attributes are determined by interviewing a sample of employees in the specific job. Each employee will be asked what behaviors contribute to success in the employee's job. The employee is also asked what behaviors do not work in the job.

    All interviewees are asked the same set of questions.
- **Develop a Long List of Key Attributes:** The behaviors received from the employee interviews are compiled and categorized under specific competencies. Based on the data received from the interviews, a grouping of competencies is given a key attribute name and description.
- **Determine Short List of Priority Key Attributes:** The Short List of Priority Key Attributes is determined by distributing the Long List of Key Attributes with descriptions to managers over the position. The managers rank the key attributes in order of importance to success in the job. When the ranking exercise is complete, the top five or six key attributes are identified as priorities for final validation.
- **Final Validation of Key Attributes:** The top five or six key attributes are then distributed to the top-level leadership team for the position. Once the leadership team approves the key attributes, the validation process is complete and the key attributes are ready to be used in the interview process.
- Interviews should take about thirty minutes to complete.
- All interviewers are asked the same set of questions.
- Thoroughly document all answers.
- If the interviewee does not have an answer to a question, you may come back to it later.
- Interviewers will be involved in developing the Long List of Key Attributes for validation.

4.2. KEY ATTRIBUTES QUESTIONNAIRE

To determine the key attributes of any job, use questions like those in Toolbox-Exhibit 4.1 to draw out the information from A Player incumbents in each position under consideration. This questionnaire was developed for a hospital client but can be easily adapted to any workplace. Try not to become so specific in your questions that you essentially prejudge what the key attributes are.

TOOLBOX-EXHIBIT 4.1. KEY ATTRIBUTES QUESTIONNAIRE

Job Category: ______________________________

Date: ________________ **Interview Done By:** ______________________

Name: ________________ **Position:** ________________________ **FT/PT**

Time in Position: _________ **Time with Hospital:** ____ **Age:** ___ **M/F**

1. **Describe the job and the tasks required of you.**

   ____

2. **Has anything changed since you were hired? If so, what, and what did you do to adapt?**

   ____

3. **What do you do each day to prepare yourself for your shift? Give an example.**

   ____

4. **Describe the aspects of your job you find most rewarding.**

   ____

5. **Describe the aspects of your job you find most difficult or challenging.**

   ____

6. **Give some characteristics you feel describe a successful _____?**

   ____

7. **Which characteristics describe an unsuccessful ___________?**

   ____

8. **How do you stay current with hospital information?**

   ____

9. **What is your approach to getting to know new coworkers? Give me an example.**

   ____

10. **Describe a difficult coworker you have had to work with. How did you handle the person?**

    ____

11. **Tell me about a time you helped a fellow coworker learn a task? What was it, and what did you do?**

    ____

12. **What do you do to make a Patient or potential Patient feel important? Give me an example.**

    ____

13. **Tell me about a difficult Patient you have had to deal with. What did you do.**

    ____

14. **Tell me about a time you did something to WOW a Patient.**

    ____

15. Tell me about a difficult event you have had to work through. What did you do?

____

16. Describe a rewarding work experience you have had recently.

____

17. What is your normal routine before you leave for the day? Give an example.

____

Thank you so much for your time and assistance.

4.3. INTERVIEW GUIDE

Toolbox-Exhibit 4.2 is an interview guide we recommend for hospital clients. It includes instructions to interviewers as well as the attributes that each interviewer is asked to interview on. Additionally, it rates people on whether or not they are an organizational match, which is a values match for the organization. The three interviewers (manager, peer, HR) will have slightly different interview guides; this is necessary in order to ensure thorough coverage of each key attribute. Once interviewers are trained with these guides, they actually result in easier and more effective interviewing because the interviewers are able to pinpoint behaviors that lead to success on the job.

TOOLBOX-EXHIBIT 4.2. *CAREPIX* INTERVIEW GUIDE

A SAMPLE FORMAT

Date ________________

Candidate ____________________ Interviewer ________________

GETTING READY

1. Review application and resume (curriculum vitae). Select jobs/experiences most pertinent to the intended job.

2. Prepare to confirm education and work history.
   a. Clarify any information you have questions about.
   b. Record any gaps in employment.

3. Review the Behavioral Questions.
   a. Become comfortable with the key attributes and their meaning.
   b. Adjust questions to better fit the candidate's work and/or school experience.

HOW TO BEGIN (TWO MINUTES)

1. Welcome the candidate and introduce yourself.

2. Explain the purpose of the interview:
   a. To become better acquainted.
   b. An opportunity to learn more about candidate's background and experience.
   c. To help candidate understand the position and organization.

3. Describe how the interview will progress:
   a. Brief review of education and jobs or experiences.
   b. Ask questions to get specific information about jobs or experiences.
   c. Provide information about the position and organization.
   d. Answer questions about the position and organization.
   e. Point out that you will both get information needed to make good decisions.
   f. Indicate you will be taking notes.
   g. Explain what happens after the interview.

4. Ask the candidate if he or she is ready to get started.

BACKGROUND CONFIRMATION (5 MINUTES)

Educational Background—seek only information not provided on application or resume (curriculum vitae).

Graduate School __________ Years ____ Degree or Major ________

College or University _______ Years ____ Degree or Major ________

Tech. School _____________ Years ____ Degree or Major ________

High School ______________ Years ____ Degree or Major ________

Work Background

Organization ____________ Position ___________Dates __________

What were or are your major responsibilities or duties? Any change in position or responsibilities?

Why did you (or why are you planning to) leave?

Organization ______________ Position _________ Dates _________

What were or are your major responsibilities or duties? Any change in position or responsibilities?

Why did you (or why are you planning to) leave?

STORY TIME (TWENTY TO THIRTY MINUTES)

Key Attribute: Getting Along with Others

Seeking opportunities to accept ideas and help from coworkers to accomplish work goals; willingness to share credit; appreciating differences in personalities; showing empathy; having a sense of humor and willingness to laugh at self.

Behavioral Questions

1. We all have bad days. Tell me a time when you had a bad day at work. What happened?
2. Have you ever worked with a team or group where one of the members was not pulling his or her weight? What did you do?
3. When you work with others, there are those that you really enjoy working with and those very few that can be a bit more difficult or challenging to get along with. Tell me about a difficult or challenging person you have worked with. What was the situation, and how did you handle it?

Beginning	Beginning
Middle	Middle
End	End
Observations: ________________	Getting Along with Others Rating: ☐

KEY ATTRIBUTE: ORGANIZATIONAL MATCH

The organization's culture is in sync with the kind of environment that satisfies personal needs; specific job duties are personally satisfying; displays a great sense of humor; demonstrates a fun yet professional nature; personifies a hard-working, "can do" attitude.

Match Questions—Ask two of these three and record the answers below.

1. {Fun & Friendly} Tell me about an organization you worked for that was or was not fun and friendly. Why did you like or dislike this?
2. {Interdepartmental Cooperation} Tell me about a time when there was or was not collaboration among departments. Did you like or dislike this?
3. {Participative Management} Tell me about a hospital you worked for where the management team did or did not help out when needed.

Where did it happen?	Where did it happen?
What did you like or dislike?	What did you like or dislike?
Why did you like or dislike it?	Why did you like or dislike it?
Observations: ____________	Hospital Match Rating: ☐

ADDITIONAL KEY ATTRIBUTES

Communication: Clearly providing information and ideas in a manner that engages the interviewer and helps him or her understand and retain the message.

Key Actions

A B C

☐ ☐ ☐ Organizes the communication

☐ ☐ ☐ Maintains interviewer's attention

☐ ☐ ☐ Adjusts to the interviewer

☐ ☐ ☐ Uses appropriate language

Communication Rating ☐

Influence – Creating a good first impression; commanding attention and respect; showing an air of confidence.

Key Actions

A B C

☐ ☐ ☐ Personal hygiene and grooming

☐ ☐ ☐ Displays professional and fun demeanor

☐ ☐ ☐ Speaks confidently and positively

☐ ☐ ☐ Maintains appropriate eye contact

Influence Rating ☐

SAYING GOOD-BYE (FIVE MINUTES)

1. Additional Information
   Make one of the following requests:
   - Describe the most important event in your education and/or work experience.
   - Tell me something about yourself that you want us to know about you.
   - Review notes.

   - Ask for response to the request.

2. Position/Organization/Location

   - Ask the candidate if he or she has any questions and note them here.

3. Say good-bye.
   - What's next.
   - Thank the candidate for coming in to interview.

WHAT TO DO AFTER THE INTERVIEW

1. Review your interview notes
   - Identify complete stories throughout CAREPix Interview Guide.
   - Place stories into appropriate key attributes.
   - Indicate whether each story is positive (+) or negative (–).
   - Consider the appropriateness of each story to the position for which the candidate is applying.
   - Determine and record the grade in the rating box (lower-right corner) for each competency. Use the following system:

Primary Ratings

A+– **Much More Than Acceptable**
(Significantly exceeds criteria for successful job performance)

A– **More Than Acceptable**
(Exceeds criteria for successful job performance)

B– **Acceptable**
(Meets criteria for successful job performance)

C– **Less Than Acceptable**
(Generally does not meet criteria for successful job performance)

Clarifying Ratings:

N/A No opportunity to observe or assess

– Weak or want more data (for example, A–, B–, C–)

1. Evaluate the candidate's observable behavior throughout the interview.
   - Review your notes and determine whether the behavior in each competency was effective (+), neutral (0), or ineffective or absent (–).
   - Place a check mark in the appropriate box for each item.
   - Use the A, B, C ratings to grade the behavior under the Communication and Influence headings on the next page. Write the grade in the box provided.
2. Complete the Interview Rating Summary Worksheet based on your interview observations.
3. Use the Interview Rating Summary Worksheet on the following page to summarize your interview ratings.

4.4. Interview Guide Matrix

The matrix in Toolbox-Table 4.1 lists the key attributes of a particular job and whose responsibility it is to determine whether applicants display those attributes. The interview guide will be adapted for each interviewer to reflect these assignments. Please note that each interviewer will be interviewing to ensure the candidate is a company match (that is, a values match) in addition to ascertaining whether the candidate has the correct attributes.

Toolbox-Table 4.1. Selection Guide Matrix

Candidate Name	**Resume Screen**	**Phone Screen**	**Human Resources**	**Lead**	**Peer**
Key Attributes			**Selection Guide #1**	**Selection Guide #2**	**Selection Guide #3**
Getting Along with Others		X	X	X	X
Winning Customers		X	X		X
Raising the Bar			X	X	
Company Match		X	X	X	
Communication	X	X	X	X	X
Influence			X	X	X

4.5. Training Guide for Values Interviewing

It's important to carefully plan your interviewer training to get maximum buy-in to the new methodology and full integration of peers in the process. The Interviewer Training Outline is an example of how a successful interviewer training can be structured.

INTERVIEWER TRAINING OUTLINE

Learning Objectives:
Upon completion of this module, participants will be able to:

- Apply the concepts of behavioral interviewing.
- Explain how to match key attributes of a candidate with the key attribute profile.
- Develop and ask behavior-based questions during the interview process.
- Use the interview guide to complete a behavior-based interview.
- Participate with an interview team in evaluating a candidate and reaching consensus on an interview decision.
- Comply with legal guidelines during an interview.

TRAINING TOPICS

1. Introduction to values- and behavior-based interviewing concepts
   a. Hiring for a values-centric culture
   b. Three common elements of credible and effective selection processes:
      i. Hire right
      ii. Fairness and consistency
      iii. Team confirmation
   c. Past behavior predicts future behavior
   d. Focus on hiring A Players

2. Best practice hiring model
   a. Recruiting strategy based on values
   b. Screen applicants by industry match
   c. Team interview includes peers
   d. Team makes hiring decision by consensus
   e. Background check
   f. Make offer

3. Concepts of key attributes
   a. Process for key attribute validation
   b. Parts of the interview guide
   c. Types of key attributes
      i. Key attributes—ability of candidate
      ii. Values-based—organizational match
   d. How key attributes are covered in the interview guide
   e. Benefits of using key attributes

4. Practice matching key attributes

5. Getting the whole story during the interview
   a. Confirm work history
   b. Past behaviors: get behavioral examples for each of the key attributes
   c. Organizational values: examples of how the candidate demonstrates the values
   d. Quest for finding behavioral examples

6. Parts of the story—beginning, middle, and end
   a. Empty stories—does not have behavioral examples
   b. Recognize "red flags" for an empty story
   c. Missing parts
   d. Practice recognizing empty stories and missing parts

7. Dig, dig, dig, and more—get to the bottom of an incomplete story
   a. Leading questions
   b. Theoretical questions
   c. Behavioral questions
   d. Practice recognizing types of questions

8. Legal guidelines—recognize and avoid illegal questions during the interview

9. How to use the interview guide to manage the interview
   a. Build rapport
   b. Take notes
   c. Cover the assigned key attributes and values

10. How to evaluate the interview based on candidate's responses—assign ratings

11. How the team consensus process works

12. Practice an interview using an interview guide

13. Practice the team consensus process

4.6. Team Consensus Worksheet

Toolbox-Table 4.2 is an example of a form that can be used by interviewers (manager, peer, and HR) as a guide for discussion of the candidates that they have all interviewed.

Toolbox-Table 4.2. Team Selection Decision Worksheet

Fill in Ratings by Each Interviewer for Each Key Attribute

Candidate Name	Human Resources	Lead	Peer
Key Attributes	Selection Guide #1	Selection Guide #2	Selection Guide #3
Getting Along with Others			
Winning Customers			
Raising the Bar			
Company Match			
Communication			
Influence			
Overall Rating			

CHAPTER 6

6.1. Values Performance Peer Review

The example in Toolbox-Exhibit 6.1 is from the early days of JetBlue. Crew members now take these surveys online, but it is an excellent example of a simple evaluation form for peer performance. The first section is aimed at encouraging cooperation; the actual evaluation of the employee's success in "Living the Values" takes place in Section II, with an overall rating of employee performance at the very end.

TOOLBOX-EXHIBIT 6.1. JETBLUE 320 REVIEW FORM

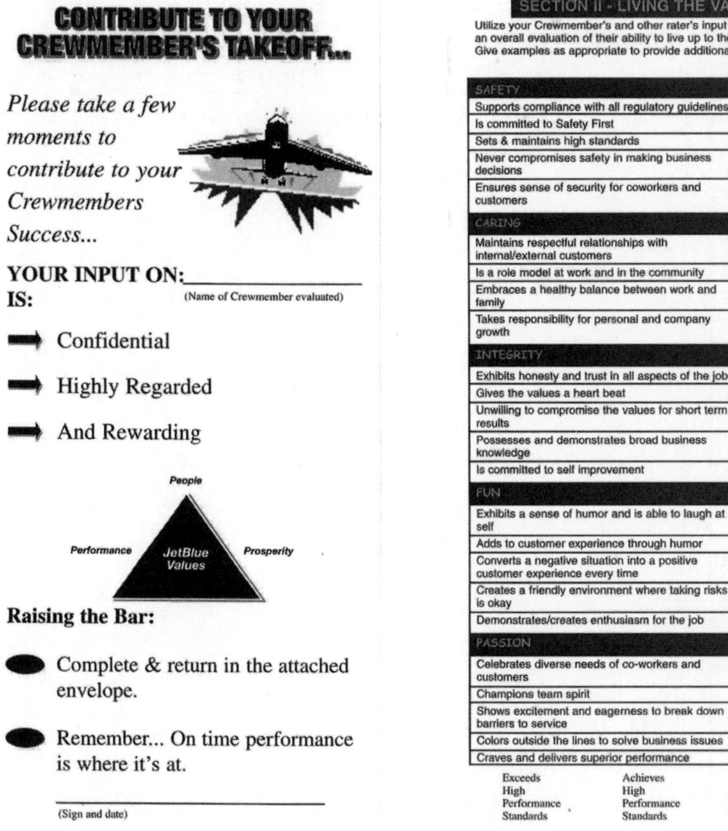

CONTRIBUTE TO YOUR CREWMEMBER'S TAKEOFF...

Please take a few moments to contribute to your Crewmembers Success...

YOUR INPUT ON: ____________ (Name of Crewmember evaluated)
IS:

- Confidential
- Highly Regarded
- And Rewarding

Raising the Bar:

- Complete & return in the attached envelope.
- Remember... On time performance is where it's at.

____
(Sign and date)

SECTION II - LIVING THE VALUES

Utilize your Crewmember's and other rater's input to compile an overall evaluation of their ability to live up to the values. Give examples as appropriate to provide additional feedback.

Below... Exceeds

SAFETY	1	2	3
Supports compliance with all regulatory guidelines			
Is committed to Safety First			
Sets & maintains high standards			
Never compromises safety in making business decisions			
Ensures sense of security for coworkers and customers			
CARING	**1**	**2**	**3**
Maintains respectful relationships with internal/external customers			
Is a role model at work and in the community			
Embraces a healthy balance between work and family			
Takes responsibility for personal and company growth			
INTEGRITY	**1**	**2**	**3**
Exhibits honesty and trust in all aspects of the job			
Gives the values a heart beat			
Unwilling to compromise the values for short term results			
Possesses and demonstrates broad business knowledge			
Is committed to self improvement			
FUN	**1**	**2**	**3**
Exhibits a sense of humor and is able to laugh at self			
Adds to customer experience through humor			
Converts a negative situation into a positive customer experience every time			
Creates a friendly environment where taking risks is okay			
Demonstrates/creates enthusiasm for the job			
PASSION	**1**	**2**	**3**
Celebrates diverse needs of co-workers and customers			
Champions team spirit			
Shows excitement and eagerness to break down barriers to service			
Colors outside the lines to solve business issues			
Craves and delivers superior performance			

Exceeds High Performance Standards — Achieves High Performance Standards — Below High Performance Standards

6.2. Values and Rewards Map

The simple grid in Toolbox-Table 6.1 shows how values can be compared against various components of employee pay and benefits programs. I encourage you to analyze your pay and benefits plans against the values in even more detail. Identify where the program design supports your organization's values and communicate this to employees.

Toolbox-Table 6.1. Values and Rewards Map

Corporate Values (samples)	Base Pay Plan	Variable Pay Plan	Traditional Benefit Pla	Nontraditional Benefit Plan
Innovation— Encouraging new ideas		Do we truly encourage and reward risk taking and new ideas?		
Integrity—Open and honest communication	Do we have transparency around our base pay structure?			
Accountability— Focus on the outcomes, not just the hours at work		Do our incentive plans truly encourage stretch performance?		Do we have programs that encourage flexible work arrangements?
Wholeness— Encourage employees to balance work and personal responsibilities			Does our medical plan provide choices to meet employee needs?	Do we offer wellness programs and encourage gym memberships? Do we provide employees with child/elder care options?

6.3. Current Compensation and Benefits Employee Survey

Toolbox-Exhibit 6.2 presents suggested questions about compensation and employee benefits that you may want to ask in focus groups or send as a survey. You should add and delete items to reflect the current state of your benefits. To attract and retain top people, we suggest that you find out which particular benefits are attractive to them. Include questions from all three sections if you want to gain a comprehensive knowledge of how valued your packages are. You may be surprised.

TOOLBOX-EXHIBIT 6.2. CURRENT COMPENSATION AND BENEFITS EMPLOYEE SURVEY

SECTION I

Do you agree with the following statements?	Agree	Not Sure	Disagree
1. My total compensation is fair for the job I do.	☺	😐	☹
2. The health benefits meet all my needs and my family's needs.	☺	😐	☹
3. I am eligible for, but do not participate in, the [company name] group medical plan.	☺	😐	☹
4. My medical copay and deductible amounts are fair.	☺	😐	☹
5. My dental copay and deductible amounts are fair.	☺	😐	☹
6. I have access to other coverage, but choose to participate in the [company name] plan.	☺	😐	☹
7. I am able to get an appointment with my doctor in a reasonable amount of time.	☺	😐	☹

Do you agree with the following statements?	Agree	Not Sure	Disagree
8. I feel the [company name] medical plan is good compared to other employers in the area.	☺	😐	☹
9. Access to specialists (cardiologist, dermatologist, and so on) is adequate.	☺	😐	☹
10. I am satisfied with the vision plan.	☺	😐	☹
11. My supervisor gives me the flexibility I need to balance work and personal time	☺	😐	☹
12. I am satisfied with the investment choices in the 401(k) plan.	☺	😐	☹

In addition to questions specific to satisfaction with the benefit programs, the survey should include questions about effectiveness of communication and understanding of the benefits programs. Demographic data (age, sex, marital status, length of service, and so on) is compiled to analyze responses by different employee groups.

SECTION II

What changes would you like to see in the current benefits plans?

___

What new benefits should be considered?

___

SECTION III

Please rate the *value*, to you, of the following programs on a scale from 1 to 4. When rating the program, consider how well it meets your needs, the ease of using the benefit, and the cost. Please check *no opinion* if you are unfamiliar with the benefit.

Program	No Value 1	Some Value 2	Good Value 3	High Value 4	No Opinion
Medical Insurance for Employee					
Medical Insurance for My Dependents					
Dental Insurance					
Vision Care Coverage					
Pharmacy Benefits					
Basic Life Insurance (provided by the company)					
Supplemental Life Insurance (additional life insurance you pay for)					
Long-Term Disability					
401(k) Plan					
Employee Assistance Program (EAP)					

6.4. Assessing Your Total Rewards Strategy

Build a total rewards graphic to better illustrate exactly how your organization is spending its people dollars and to allow for a discussion of desired changes. To create the total view of the rewards expense allocation for your organization, you will need to work with your controller/finance group to gather the current annual company expense for each of your current rewards programs. Your organization may use a "benefits cost assumption" reflected as a percent of payroll (for example, 30 percent). Ask for the detail behind this assumption, which should include the items shown in Toolbox-Exhibit 6.3. Be sure to include all expenses: for example, medical plan costs should include the cost of third-party administration (TPA) if your organization is self-insured.

TOOLBOX-EXHIBIT 6.3. ASSESSING YOUR TOTAL REWARDS STRATEGY

COMPONENT	ANNUAL COMPANY COST (last fiscal year)	PERCENT OF TOTAL
CASH COMPENSATION		
Total Base Pay		
Total Variable Pay		
HEALTH & WELFARE Plans		
Group Medical Plan(s)	*(DO NOT INCLUDE EMPLOYEE CONTRIBUTIONS)*	
Group Dental Plan(s)		
Vision Plan(s)		
Prescription Drug Plan (if separate from medical)		
Life insurance: basic, supplemental and dependent/spouse coverage		
Long-Term Disability		
Short-Term Disability		
Employee Assistance Plan		
RETIREMENT PLANS		
401(k) Plan (include company contributions and all administration costs)		
Pension Plan (include company contributions and all administration costs)		
Profit-Sharing Plan		

6.5. Nontraditional Benefits Chart

Toolbox-Exhibit 6.4 presents some nontraditional benefits that you may want to have your employees rate in terms of importance. Our clients have been surprised by some of the answers.

TOOLBOX-EXHIBIT 6.4. THE CULTURE: CREATING THE EMPLOYEE EXPERIENCE

THE CULTURE: Creating the Employee Experience		
Work/Life Balance	**Acknowledgment and Recognition**	**Learning and Development**
Wellness Benefits	Paid Time Away from Work	Scholarships for Dependents
Health Fair/Screening on-site	Attendance Recognition	Education Assistance
Job Share Arrangements	Stored Value Cards	ESL class on-site/paid
PTO Banks	Profit-Sharing	Financial Planning
Adoption Assistance	Accrued Sick Days	Cross-Training
Credit Union/Banking Services Access	Life Days/Volunteering	Walk in My Shoes Day
Catastrophic Fund	Floating Holidays	Library/Book Loan
Company Loans	Tickets to Events (Sports/Theatre/Fine Arts)	Voter Registration on Site
Child/Elder Care Assistance	Service Awards	Parenting Seminars
Home Purchase Assistance	Logo Item Awards	Industry Business Seminars
Auto Repair/Wash/Maint. on Site	Company Events	Culinary Classes
Bicycle Rental/Parking Repair	Employee Named Items on Property	Marine Biology Learning
Take-Home Meals	"Full" Access to Spa Services	Sabbaticals
Legal Assistance	Family Events at Work	Personal Safety Training
Funeral Reimbursement	Family Access to Hotel Services	Kids' Summer Camp
Transit/Parking Subsidies	Employee Entrance Design	PC Classes
Pet Insurance	Great Break Areas	"Partner" with Local Community Colleges
Group Auto/ Homeowners Ins.	Employee Locker Areas	
Alternative Medicine Coverage		
Domestic Partner Benefits		

CHAPTER 8

8.1. Sample Values Communications Plan

Plan how you will continually communicate around the values, both in words and in other ways. Toolbox-Exhibit 8.1 presents just a short sample; you should include all significant upcoming changes.

TOOLBOX-EXHIBIT 8.1. SAMPLE VALUES COMMUNICATIONS PLAN

Values Communication Plan

KEY MESSAGES

1. Link the core values to our historic mission and to our vision
2. Explain the inclusive, participatory processes for selecting core values
3. Explain values/definitions and indicate relationship between values and behaviors
4. Stress that this is clarification and enhancement not a "new program"
5. Show the connection to practical "people processes"
6. Show linkage to other initiatives such as Innovating Excellence

WHEN	WHERE	WHO	BY WHOM	WHAT	HOW
Dates/Frequency	Venue	Target Audience	Responsible	Specific Messages	Aids & Tools
Quarterly 12/12/07	Board of Trustees Mtgs	Board of Trustees	Gerald W	• Opportunities for Board leadership	
10/1/07 10/2/07 9/28/07 10/16/07	1:1 meetings	Senior Vice Presidents: Danny Fontoura Michael Jackson Zareh Sarrafian Liz Dickinson	Gerald W	• Inclusion of values in senior leadership decisions • Use of values in performance evaluation of senior leadership	
Bi/weekly 10/9/07 10/25/07 11/7/07	Operations Committee Meetings	Operations Committee	Gerald W	• Inclusion of values in administration decisions • Use of values in performance evaluations of all administration employees	
Quarterly 11/15/07	Dept Head meetings	Departments heads	Gerald W	• Role of department heads in communicating values • Task of department heads in "people processes"	
Monthly 12/19/07	ECH Leadership Meeting	ECH leaders	Gerald W	• Role of leaders in communicating values • Task of leaders in "people processes"	
	CH Leadership	CH leaders	Gerald W Betsy Tan	• Role of leaders in communicating values • Task of leaders in "people processes"	
10/31/07	UHC Executive Directors	UHC leaders	Gerald W	• Possible alignment of values with LLUMC values	
Monthly Semi-annual Quarterly Weekly Monthly Monthly Monthly 1/23/08 11/27/08	PWET meetings Resident Dir Retreat Pipeline e/news Residents newsletter PPAC SM Dean newsletter Medical Staff Exec Mtg ECH Clinical Council ECH Physicians & Leadership Retreat	Physicians	Gerald W Gina M		

CHAPTER 9

9.1. Annual Values Team Review Checklist

With the simple checklist in Toolbox-Table 9.1, your Values Team can determine how far along on your values journey you are and who will be responsible for further progress. As with most things, assigning specific responsibilities to individuals or teams works wonders in getting the job done.

Toolbox-Table 9.1. Annual Values Review Checklist

Review Item	Recommendation Action and Date	Assigned To
1. Core Values have been established and are recognized by every department of the organization.		
2. Core Values drive decisions made by the organization at all levels.		
3. Every employee within the organization can state the Values from memory.		
4. Specific behaviors have been assigned to the Core Values.		
5. Behavior-based Values are integrated into the hiring process.		
6. Behavior-based Values are integrated into the performance planning and appraizal process.		
7. The organization makes hiring decisions based on Values.		
8. The organization makes firing decisions based on Values.		
9. The organization provides recognition and rewards based on Values.		

9.2. P.F. Chang's Board Evaluation for CEO

The board of directors of P.F. Chang's evaluates its CEO yearly, an evaluation that explicitly includes questions about the values all P.F. Chang's employees are expected to display (see Toolbox-Exhibit 9.1). Powerful stuff.

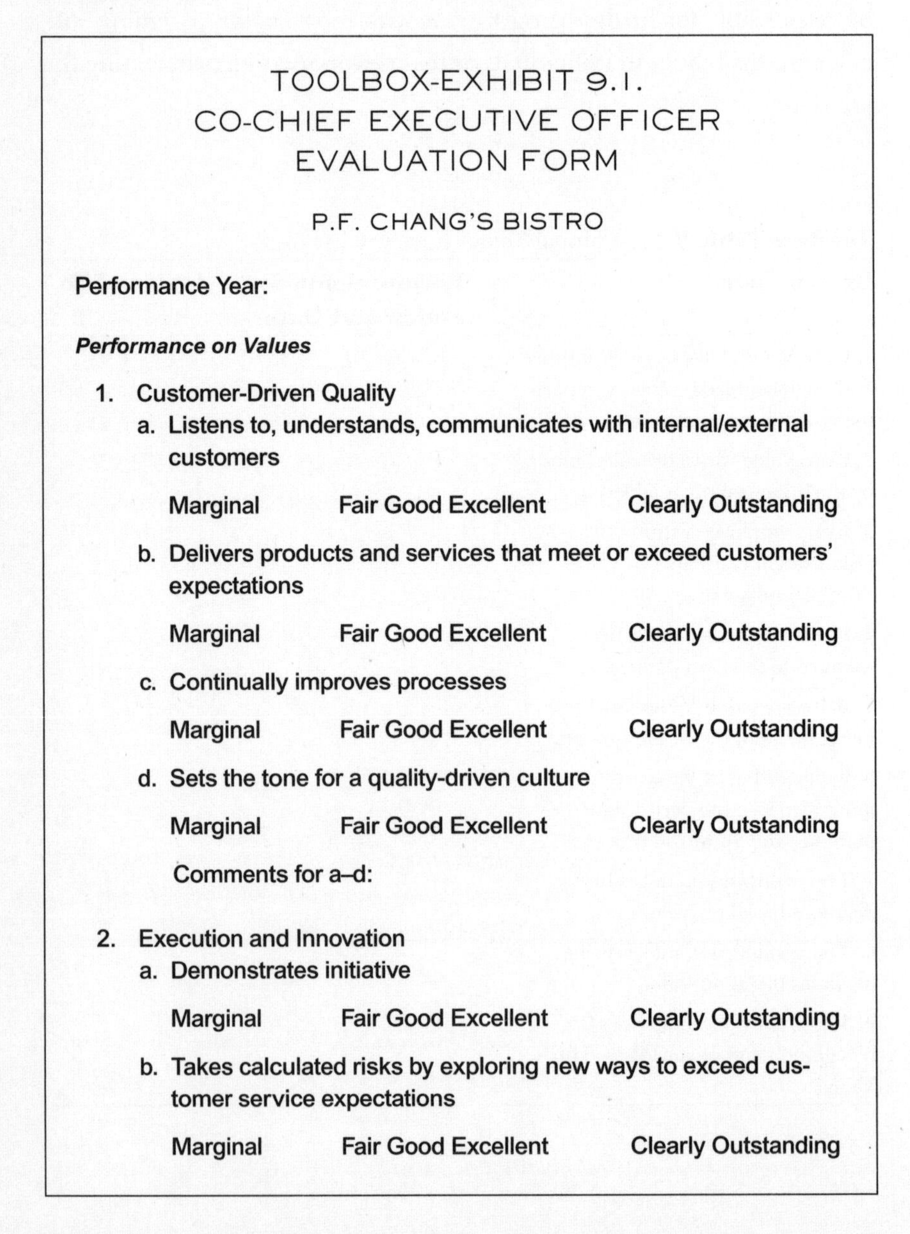

TOOLBOX-EXHIBIT 9.1.
CO-CHIEF EXECUTIVE OFFICER
EVALUATION FORM

P.F. CHANG'S BISTRO

Performance Year:

Performance on Values

1. Customer-Driven Quality
   a. Listens to, understands, communicates with internal/external customers

      Marginal Fair Good Excellent Clearly Outstanding

   b. Delivers products and services that meet or exceed customers' expectations

      Marginal Fair Good Excellent Clearly Outstanding

   c. Continually improves processes

      Marginal Fair Good Excellent Clearly Outstanding

   d. Sets the tone for a quality-driven culture

      Marginal Fair Good Excellent Clearly Outstanding

   Comments for a–d:

2. Execution and Innovation
   a. Demonstrates initiative

      Marginal Fair Good Excellent Clearly Outstanding

   b. Takes calculated risks by exploring new ways to exceed customer service expectations

      Marginal Fair Good Excellent Clearly Outstanding

c. Executes effectively

Marginal Fair Good Excellent Clearly Outstanding

d. Fosters innovation and creative thinking

Marginal Fair Good Excellent Clearly Outstanding

Comments for a–d:

3. Stewardship

a. Assumes responsibility and accountability for results

Marginal Fair Good Excellent Clearly Outstanding

b. Improves own knowledge, skills, behaviors, and competencies

Marginal Fair Good Excellent Clearly Outstanding

c. Supports the development of our staff

Marginal Fair Good Excellent Clearly Outstanding

d. Helps transform P.F. Chang's into a vigorous organization that creates value for all stakeholders

Marginal Fair Good Excellent Clearly Outstanding

Comments for a–d:

4. Teamwork

a. Supports team and group efforts

Marginal Fair Good Excellent Clearly Outstanding

b. Shares knowledge and information with board

Marginal Fair Good Excellent Clearly Outstanding

c. Respects ideas and diversity of colleagues

Marginal Fair Good Excellent Clearly Outstanding

d. Respects ideas and diversity of board members

Marginal Fair Good Excellent Clearly Outstanding

e. Assumes different responsibilities to help team meet its goals

Marginal Fair Good Excellent Clearly Outstanding

Comments for a–e:

NOTES

Introduction

1. Goodison, Donna. "Branson: U.S. Airlines Need Shaking Up." *Boston Herald* Business section, February 12, 2009, p. 29.
2. Rigby, Darrell. "Look Before You Lay Off." *Harvard Business Review* [http://hbr.org/2002/04/look-before-you-lay-off/ar/1], April 2002.

Chapter One

1. Kanter, Rosabeth Moss. "Transforming Giants." *Harvard Business School, The Centennial Business Summit,* Summit Report, 2008, p. 2.
2. Vickers, Mark, and others. "Cultivating Effective Corporate Cultures: A Global Study of Challenges and Strategies: Current Trends and Future Possibilities, 2008–2018." American Management Association, 2008, p. vi.
3. Burt, Ron. "When Is Corporate Culture a Competitive Asset?" *Financial Times,* November 1, 1999, pp. 14–15.
4. Espinoza, Javier. "Culture Change Is the Final Frontier." *WSJ.com* [http://online.wsj.com/article/SB100014240527487037873045750753816641 89008.html], February 23, 2010.
5. Peterson, Joel, JetBlue and Peterson Partners. Personal interview, April 26, 2010.
6. McFarland, Keith. "Why Zappos Offers New Hires $2000 to Quit." *Businessweek.com* [http://www.businessweek.com/smallbiz/content/sep2008/sb20080916_288698.htm?campaign_id=rss_smlbz], September 16, 2008.

7. Trainor, Len. Heritage Home Healthcare. Personal interview, December 4, 2009.
8. Winslow, Gerald, Loma Linda University Medical Center. Personal interview, November 19, 2009.
9. Pryne, Eric. "Starbucks Chief Rises to the Top." *Seattle Times* [http://seattletimes.nwsource.com/html/businesstechnology/2012136200_ceotopfive20.html], June 19, 2010.

Chapter Two

1. Rosenthal, Jeff, and Masarech, Mary Ann. "High Performance Cultures: How Values Can Drive Business Results." *Journal of Organizational Excellence*, February 12, 2003, *22*(2), p. 3.
2. Peterson, Joel, JetBlue and Peterson Partners. Personal interview, April 26, 2010.
3. Freiburg, Jackie and Kevin. *Nuts! Southwest Airlines' Crazy Recipe for Business and Personal Success.* New York: Broadway Books, 1998, pp. 144–45.
4. Starbucks Mission Statement [www.starbucks.com/about-us/company-information/mission-statement].
5. Edmonds, Chris, and Glaser, Bob. "Culture by Default or by Design?" *Talent Management Magazine.* January 2010, p. 38.
6. Stamoulis, Dean. "Corporate Culture Is Becoming a Science." *Forbes.com* [http://www.forbes.com/2009/11/23/corporate-culture-science-leadership-governance-succession.html], November 23, 2009, p. 1.
7. Dodds, Sheryl. Florida Hospitals. Personal interview, April 27, 2010.
8. Lagace, Martha. "Corporate Values and Employee Cynicism." *Harvard Business School Working Knowledge* [http://hbswk.hbs.edu/item/5229.html], February 27, 2006, p. 3.

Chapter Three

1. Welch, Jack and Suzy. "Values Are the How of a Firm's Mission, the Key to Winning." *livemint.com* [http://www.livemint.com/2009/10/04224616/Values-are-the-how-of-a-firm.html], October 5, 2009.
2. Aspen Institute. FIELD program. "The Organizational Foundations of Sustainability." *FIELD Forum,* July 2009, 23, p. 3.
3. Haines, Anne, ACCION New Mexico*Arizona*Colorado. Personal interview, April 30, 2010.

4. Rice, Steven, Juniper Networks. Personal interview, May 4, 2010.
5. Peterson, Joel, JetBlue and Peterson Partners. Personal interview, April 26, 2010.
6. Rice interview.
7. Ibid.

Chapter Four

1. Haines, Anne, ACCION New Mexico*Arizona*Colorado. Personal interview, April 30, 2010.
2. Huselid, Mark A., Beatty, Richard W., and Becker, Brian E. "'A Players' or 'A Positions'? The Strategic Logic of Workforce Management." *Harvard Business Review*, December 2005, p. 2.
3. Denham, Charles, M.D., and Rhoades, Ann. Patient Safety Conference, West Penn Allegheny Health System, Pittsburgh, October 22, 2009.
4. Clifford, Stephanie. "The New Science of Hiring." *Inc.com* [www.inc.com/magazine/20060801], August 1, 2006.
5. Ibid.
6. Keith, Camille, Camille Keith Associates. Personal interview, April 30, 2010.
7. Easdown, L. Jane., and others. "The Behavioral Interview, a Method to Evaluate ACGME Competencies in Resident Selection: A Pilot Project." *Journal of Education in Perioperative Medicine*, 2005, *7*(1), January-June, pp. 4–5.

Chapter Five

1. Gittell, Jody Hoffer. *The Southwest Airlines Way: Using the Power of Relationships to Achieve High Performance.* New York: McGraw-Hill, 2005, p. 19.
2. Maurister, Rob, JetBlue Airways. Personal interview, June 11, 2010.
3. Denham, Charles, M.D. Health Care Concepts Corporation (HCC) and Texas Medical Institute of Technology (TMIT). Personal interview, May 17, 2010.
4. Barger, Dave, JetBlue Airways. Personal interviews, April 9, 2010 and May 13, 2010.
5. Kelman, Glenn, Redfin.com. Personal interview, May 20, 2010.
6. Pfeffer, Jeffrey, and Sutton, Robert I. "Evidence-Based Management." *Harvard Business Review*, January 2006, Reprint R0601E, pp. 2, 11.

Chapter Six

1. Larson, Jennifer. "Maritz Poll: Bosses Not 'On the Same Page' as Employees Regarding Recognition" [http://www.maritz.com/Maritz-Poll/2006/Maritz-Poll-Bosses-Not-On-the-Same-Page-as-Employees-Regarding-Recognition.aspx], January 25, 2006.
2. Winslow, Gerald, Loma Linda University Medical Center. Personal interview, November 19, 2009.
3. Barger, Dave, JetBlue Airways. Personal interviews, April 9, 2010 and May 13, 2010.
4. Axelrod, Beth, Handfield-Jones, Helen, and Michaels, Ed. "A New Game Plan for C Players." *Harvard Business Review, On Point* (reprint product 8598), January 2002, p. 9.

Chapter Seven

1. Vickers, Mark, and others. "Cultivating Effective Corporate Cultures: A Global Study of Challenges and Strategies: Current Trends and Future Possibilities, 2008–2018." American Management Association, 2008, pp. 24–5.
2. Barger, Dave, JetBlue Airways. Personal interview, April 9, 2010.
3. Ibid.
4. Huseman, Richard C., Bilbrey, Pamela, and Jones, Brian. "Coaching for Great Leadership in Health Care." *BLI White Papers.* The Baptist Health Care Leadership Institute, 2007, pp. 13–14.
5. Peterson, Joel, JetBlue and Peterson Partners. Personal interview, April 26, 2010.
6. Drucker, Peter. *Managing the Non-Profit Organization.* Oxford: Butterworth Heineman, 1990.
7. Kelleher, Rick, Pyramid Hotels. Personal interview, June 3, 2010.
8. Ibid.
9. "Meet the Top Small Company Workplaces of 2010." *Inc.com* [www.inc.com/top-workplaces/2010/meet-the-top-small-company-workplaces-of-2010.html], June 8, 2010.

Chapter Eight

1. Towers Watson. "Capitalizing on Effective Communication: How Courage, Innovation and Discipline Drive Business Results in Challenging Times." 2009/2010 Communication ROI Study Report, 2009, p. 2.

2. Barger, Dave, JetBlue Airways. Personal interview, May 13, 2010.
3. Towers Watson, "Capitalizing on Effective Communication," p. 10.
4. Yates, Jon. "Customers Get Results by Tweeting Discontent." *Chicago Tribune* business section, May 10, 2010, p. 22.
5. Kelman, Glenn, Redfin.com. Personal interview, May 20, 2010.
6. Rice, Steven, Juniper Networks. Personal interview, May 4, 2010.
7. Urban, Glen L. "The Trust Imperative." MIT Sloan School of Management, Working Paper 4302–03, March 2003, p. 6.
8. Federico, Rick, P.F. Chang's China Bistro. Personal interview, June 10, 2010.
9. Miller, Jason. "Pei Wei WOW's a Guest—The Power of Social Media." Private e-mail message to Rick Federico, March 5, 2010.
10. Kelleher, Rick, Pyramid Hotels. Personal interview, June 3, 2010.

Chapter Nine

1. Cohn, Jeffrey M., Khurana, Rakesh, and Reeves, Laura. "Growing Talent as if Your Business Depended on It." *Harvard Business Review,* October 2005, p. 33.
2. Rice, Christopher. "Four Priorities: Build Bonds with Stakeholders." BlessingWhite white paper [www.blessingwhite.com/Content/Articles/Rice%20March%202007%20LE%20Article%20Four%20Priorities.pdf], 2007.
3. Quaid, Dennis, Thao, Julie, and Denham, Charles, M.D. "Story Power: The Secret Weapon." *Journal of Patient Safety,* March 2010, *6*(1).

REFERENCES

Aspen Institute. FIELD program, "The Organizational Foundations of Sustainability." *FIELD Forum*, Issue 23, July 2009.

Barger, Dave. JetBlue Airways, personal interviews, April 9, 2010 and May 13, 2010.

Burt, Ron. "When is Corporate Culture a Competitive Asset?" *Financial Times*. November 1, 1999.

Clifford, Stephanie. "The New Science of Hiring." Inc.com. [www.inc.com/magazine/20060801]. August 1, 2006.

Cohn, Jeffrey M., Khurana, Rakesh, and Reeves, Laura. "Growing Talent as if Your Business Depended on It." *Harvard Business Review*, October 2005.

Cornejo, T. J. "12/14/09." Private e-mail message to Mark Kirke, December 25, 2009.

Denham, Charles, M.D. Health Care Concepts Corporation (HCC) and Texas Medical Institute of Technology (TMIT). Personal interview, May 17, 2010.

Denham, Charles, M.D., and Rhoades, Ann. Patient Safety Conference, West Penn Allegheny Health System, Pittsburgh, PA, October 22, 2009.

Dodds, Sheryl. Florida Hospitals. Personal interview, April 27, 2010.

Drucker, Peter. *Managing the Non-Profit Organization*. Oxford: Butterworth Heineman, 1990.

Easdowne, L. Jane, and others. "The Behavioral Interview, A Method to Evaluate ACGME Competencies in Resident Selection: A Pilot Project." *Journal of Education in Perioperative Medicine*, 7(1), January–June 2005.

Edmonds, Chris, and Glaser, Bob. "Culture by Default or by Design?" *Talent Management*, January 2010.

Espinoza, Javier. "Culture Change Is the Final Frontier." WSJ.com. [http://online.wsj.com/article/SB10001424052748703787304575075381664189008.html]. February 23, 2010.

Federico, Rick. P.F. Chang's China Bistro. Personal interview, June 10, 2010.

Fisk, Margaret Cronin, Sullivan, Brian K., and Freifield, Karen. "Mine Owner's CEO Fought Regulators, Town, Even Maid." Bloomberg.com. [http://www.bloomberg.com/news/2010-04-09/massey-s-blankenship-fought-regulators-town-as-coal-mine-operator-s-chief.html]. April 9, 2010.

Freiburg, Jackie and Kevin. *Nuts! Southwest Airlines' Crazy Recipe for Business and Personal Success*. New York: Broadway Books, 1998.

Gittell, Jody Hoffer. *The Southwest Airlines Way: Using the Power of Relationships to Achieve High Performance*. New York: McGraw-Hill, 2005.

Goodison, Donna. "Branson: U.S. Airlines Need Shaking Up." *Boston Herald*, February 12, 2009.

Haines, Ann. ACCION New Mexico*Arizona*Colorado. Personal interview, April 30, 2010.

Huselid, Mark A., Beatty, Richard W., and Becker, Brian E. "'A Players' or 'A Positions'? The Strategic Logic of Workforce Management." *Harvard Business Review*, December 2005.

Huseman, Richard C., Bilbrey, Pamela, and Jones, Brian. "Coaching for Great Leadership in Health Care." BLI White Papers, The Baptist Health Care Leadership Institute, 2007.

Kanter, Rosabeth Moss. *SuperCorp: How Vanguard Companies Create Innovation, Profits, Growth, and Social Good*. New York: Crown Business, 2009.

———. "SuperCorp: Values as Guidance System." *Harvard Business School Working Knowledge*, August 24, 2009.

———. "Transforming Giants." Harvard Business School, The Centennial Business Summit, Summit Report, 2008.

Keith, Camille. Camille Keith Associates. Personal interview. April 30, 2010.

Kelleher, Rick. Pyramid Hotels. Personal interview, June 3, 2010.

Kelman, Glenn. Redfin.com. Personal interview, May 20, 2010.

Lagace, Martha. "Corporate Values and Employee Cynicism." *Harvard Business School Working Knowledge*. [http://hbswk.hbs.edu/item/5229.html]. February 27, 2006.

Larson, Jennifer. "Maritz Poll: Bosses Not 'On the Same Page' as Employees Regarding Recognition." [http://www.maritz.com/Maritz-Poll/2006/Maritz-Poll-Bosses-Not-On-the-Same-Page-as-Employees-Regarding-Recognition.aspx]. January 25, 2006.

Maurister, Rob. JetBlue Airways. Personal interview, June 11, 2010.

McFarland, Keith. "Why Zappos Offers New Hires $2000 to Quit." Businessweek.com. [http://www.businessweek.com/smallbiz/content/sep2008/sb20080916_288698.htm?campaign_id=rss_smlbz]. September 16, 2008.

"Meet the Top Small Company Workplaces of 2010." Inc.com. [www.inc.com/top-workplaces/2010/meet-the-top-small-company-workplaces-of-2010.html]. June 8, 2010.

Miller, Jason. "Pei Wei WOW's a Guest—The Power of Social Media." Private e-mail message to Rick Federico, March 5, 2010.

Peterson, Joel. JetBlue and Peterson Partners. Personal interview, April 26, 2010.

Pfeffer, Jeffrey, and Sutton, Robert I. "Evidence-Based Management." *Harvard Business Review*, January 2006, Reprint R0601E.

Quaid, Dennis, Thao, Julie, and Denham, Charles, M.D. "Story Power: The Secret Weapon." *Journal of Patient Safety*, *6*(1), March 2010.

Rice, Christopher. "Four Priorities: Build Bonds with Stakeholders." BlessingWhite white paper [www.blessingwhite.com/Content/Articles/Rice%20March%202007%20LE%20Article%20Four%20Priorities.pdf]. 2007.

Rice, Steven. Juniper Networks. Personal interview, May 4, 2010.

Rigby, Darrell. "Look Before You Lay Off." *Harvard Business Review*. [http://hbr.org/2002/04/look-before-you-lay-off/ar/1]. April 2002.

Rosenthal, Jeff, and Masarech, Mary Ann. "High Performance Cultures: How Values Can Drive Business Results." *Journal of Organizational Excellence*, *22*(2), February 12, 2003.

Sage, Alexandria, and Stempel, Jonathan. "Lawsuit Exposes Wal-Mart to Billions in Potential Damages." Reuters.com. [www.reuters.com/article/idUSTRE63P42920100427]. April 27, 2010.

Stamoulis, Dean. "Corporate Culture Is Becoming a Science." Forbes.com. [http://www.forbes.com/2009/11/23/corporate-culture-science-leadership-governance-succession.html]. November 23, 2009.

Starbucks mission statement. [www.starbucks.com/about-us/company-information/mission-statement].

Towers Watson. "Capitalizing on Effective Communication: How Courage, Innovation and Discipline Drive Business Results in Challenging Times." 2009/2010 Communication ROI Study Report, 2009.

Trainor, Len. Heritage Home Healthcare. Personal interview, December 4, 2009.

Urban, Glen L. "The Trust Imperative," MIT Sloan School of Management, Working Paper 4302–03, March 2003.

Vickers, Mark, and others. "Cultivating Effective Corporate Cultures: A Global Study of Challenges and Strategies: Current Trends and Future Possibilities, 2008–2018." American Management Association, 2008.

Welch, Jack and Suzy. "Values Are the How of a Firm's Mission, the Key to Winning." livemint.com. [http://www.livemint.com/2009/10/04224616/Values-are-the-how-of-a-firm.html]. October 5, 2009.

Winslow, Gerald. Loma Linda University Hospitals. Personal interview, November 19, 2009.

Yates, Jon. "Customers Get Results by Tweeting Discontent." *Chicago Tribune*, May 10, 2010.

ACKNOWLEDGMENTS

Oftentimes I read acknowledgments and wonder whether all the people thanked really contributed as much as is implied. In my case, this book simply would not be a reality without the help of my partners and the great leaders I have been so blessed to have worked with over the years. You asked me, just often enough, "When are you going to put all this stuff into a book?" and so I have. My goal is to expose as many people as possible to a way of leadership that really has positive benefits for everyone who tries it.

I would like to express my thanks to a number of people who helped make this book possible. I am deeply grateful to:

- My partners at People Ink. This book truly would not have happened without you. You are simply the best people and most customer-centric players I have ever had the pleasure of working with. Thank you for the many years of working and playing together. Linde Harned, Shelley Wells, Delise Crimmins, and Jeff Sullivan are original VPs (Visionary People) with People Ink and were critical to the development of the Values Blueprint model and the entire system we use today. Gayle Watson, Julie Brown, and Shannon Mick are partners who have been instrumental in implementing and further refining this model within health care and other venues. I owe tons of gratitude to MOP (Manager of People) Sherry Roberts, who always tells me where to be and when to be there and sometimes even how to behave! And to the thousands who now work at companies where the Values Blueprint has been implemented, I want to thank you for being A Players every day.

- My values-centric colleagues and clients who contributed their stories and insights to the book. Those who gave generously of their time include Dave Barger of JetBlue, Sheryl Dodds of Florida Hospitals, Rick Federico of P.F. Chang's China Bistro, Anne Haines of ACCION New Mexico*Arizona*Colorado, Camille Keith of Camille Keith Associates and former VP of Southwest Airlines, Rick Kelleher of Pyramid Hotels and former CEO of Doubletree Hotels, Glenn Kelman of Redfin .com, Rob Maruster of JetBlue, Joel Peterson of JetBlue, Steve Rice of Juniper Networks, D. F. "Duffy" Swan of French Family of Companies, Len Trainor of Heritage Home Healthcare, and Gerald Winslow of Loma Linda University Medical Center. You are living examples of an authentic servant leadership that I will always try to emulate, and you have my appreciation and gratitude on a daily basis.
- My agent, Linda Konner, and my writing partner, Nancy Shepherdson. I love you both and would not have come this far without you. You are the best.
- My editor and friend, Karen Murphy of Jossey-Bass. I appreciate all of your support in making this dream come true.
- My partner in health care, Dr. Charles Denham, for introducing me to some of the most values-driven caregivers in the world. I am also thankful to him for being an early advocate of writing my ideas down in book form so that more people could profit from them.
- My friend and gone-too-soon colleague, Captain Terry "Moose" Millard, who gave many of these ideas early written form and who will always remain in my heart as a hero. Moose would have loved to have seen this book on the shelves.

- My parents, Lena and Doc Weiler, who taught me what it means to live values every day.
- My brothers, Jim, Greg, and Jeff, and sisters, Caroline, Cindy, and Elaine, who taught me the value of fun and family.
- My husband, best friend, and biggest supporter, Russ. Thank you so much for never saying a word about the time it took to make this book a reality.

ABOUT THE AUTHORS

Ann Rhoades has been practicing values-based leadership for over twenty-five years. *Built on Values* is based on her experience developing companies, such as JetBlue Airways and Southwest Airlines, that are celebrated as much for their values-based, people-centric cultures (both employees and customers) as they are for their excellent products and service. As president of Albuquerque-based People Ink, she helps clients build values-based corporate cultures, using the Values Blueprint principles. Her clients have included Disney, Jenny Craig, Exxon, WestJet, Pebble Beach, SunTrust, Dave & Buster's, Cranium, Morton's Steakhouse, Campbell's Soup Company, QuikTrip, Florida Hospital System, Loma Linda University Medical Center Hospital, French Family of Companies, Juniper Networks, and Regent Surgical Health. She is also CEO of CareLeaders, LLC, a company that provides leadership, workforce, and patient-centered care solutions for the health care industry.

As one of the five founding executives of JetBlue Airways, Ann Rhoades guided the first executive team through creating a Values Blueprint, which now defines the JetBlue culture. Before JetBlue, Rhoades was chief people officer for Southwest Airlines during the airline's growth period. While at Southwest, she was instrumental in establishing the Culture Committee, which still operates today to oversee the Southwest Airlines culture. Previously, Rhoades was executive vice president of team services at Doubletree and Promus Hotel Corporations.

Today she continues to serve on the JetBlue board of directors as well as on the boards of P.F. Chang's China Bistro; HireVue, Inc.; Anderson School of Business at the University of New Mexico; and ACCION New Mexico*Arizona*Colorado, and she is board chair of Safer New Mexico Now. She serves on the executive council for Brigham and Women's Hospital at Harvard Medical School. She has also served on the boards of Restoration Hardware and Albuquerque Community Foundation. Ann received an MBA in management from the University of New Mexico.

For the past ten years, Rhoades has been a keynote speaker for large business conferences across the globe on the Values Blueprint principles. For more information, please visit www.peopleink.com or builtonvaluesbook.com.

Nancy Shepherdson is a freelance journalist who has written more than five hundred articles and five books over the past twenty years. Her most recent ghostwritten book is *Trust: The Secret Weapon of Effective Business Leaders*, published by St. Martin's Press in 2007. Her work focuses primarily on business and consumer issues, often with a contrarian bent. Her byline has appeared in a variety of well-known magazines, including the *Los Angeles Times Magazine*, *Continental*, *Newsweek Japan*, *Sierra*, *American Heritage*, *Woman's Day*, and *Boys' Life*. In addition, she has also contributed to many business trade publications, including *Bank Marketing*, *Professional Collector*, *Business Ingenuity*, and *Contract Professional* magazines. Shepherdson has an MBA in marketing and finance from Northwestern University and an MA in economics from the University of Michigan.

INDEX